Memoirs o

B. A. Hunter

In loving memory of James Brady Grissom

1927-2017

May the Almighty forever keep you in His loving grace…

One

"Shoo! Would you go on?" I was thirteen, riding

around in the fields behind our house on my horse
Taleramus while Valdez, the younger of the two horses,
kept coming up from behind wanting to play.

The horse always did that. The two horses were
inseparable and anytime I went out riding on Taleramus
he would always tag along, sometimes coming up to nip
on Taleramus' rear. It always scared me. I had these
visions run through my head of Taleramus forgetting all
about me and running off with the other horse while I
attempted to hold on for dear life.

I used to try to lock the younger horse up, but he
had long since grown wise to all my tricks. Nothing, not

even treats, worked for very long. My only option was then to deal with it and keep Talermaus at a steady trot.

"Oh!" I complained as I looked forward again to veer around a tree in my path.

"April!" I remember hearing off in the distance. It was my mother, Cynthia, calling me. I had ridden much too long that day, and my mother had already been expecting me home for a good forty-five minutes.

My mother Cynthia was on her third husband at this point in her life. She had me when she was about twenty years old when she was married to my father, Lenard, her first husband.

My mother's second marriage was very short-lived, but it nonetheless produced my second brother, Richard. Her second husband ended up disappearing on her one day when my brother Richard was only a baby. She eventually went on to divorce him and marry Geoffrey, her third husband, whom she was still with at this particular point in my life.

This third marriage produced my youngest brother, Joseph. It wasn't to be happily-ever-after, however, as my mother would then go on a few years later to marry her fourth husband, Wallace. That marriage would produce my sisters, two identical twin girls, from whom I would be over twenty years apart in age.

My parents had divorced when I was only about two years old, and they spent my entire childhood doing nothing but fighting each other- both in and out of court- and talking bad about one another.

I spent the majority of the time when I was about six to thirteen years old living with my father, Lenard. I moved to live with my mother when I got a bit older, and I found it extremely difficult to make friends.

It's true; I was always the socially awkward one in school. When we'd pair off into teams during PE, I was always the last one to be picked, and even then I'm certain I was only picked because I was the last available option.

Despite my social awkwardness and difficulty making friends, however, I did love the physical location where I lived with my mother as a teenager. My maternal grandparents had a nice house and several acres of land located right on the lake. I lived there with my mother, brothers, and stepdad in a separate house on the other side of the property.

I think what probably made my life more bearable during those years was the presence of my grandmother, Loretta, whom I referred to as "Nana." It was often her that gave me the most solace during this time in my life. She was always a very soft-spoken and kind-hearted woman. Even in the most difficult times she always had a way of remaining calm about the situation.

My years there with my mother probably would have ended up being much worse for me if it had not been for her presence in my life and gentle kindness. Though I always loved my mother, we did not always get along well. I oftentimes had a strained relationship with her growing up.

My mother always led what I considered to be a hectic lifestyle from all her various marriages, constant relocating and job-switching. She even became the primary breadwinner in her third marriage for a time while my stepdad, Geoffrey, went to college to get a nursing degree.

As far as my father, Lenard, he always had what I believed to be very narcissistic tendencies and was a massive control-freak. Unlike some, however, his self-image had apparently never been all that important to him. Even when I was a child, he always lived in an old worn-down trailer house. A college drop-out, he always worked in the same dead-end job, all the while complaining about how he'd find a different line of work eventually.

Despite my socially awkward ways growing up, there was one friendship that always stood the test of time. In the third grade, I met Sheila. Sheila was actually about a year older than me but had been held back a grade, apparently, when she was younger. We hit it off immediately and became friends. We were always together. Either she would be coming to stay over at my house, or I would be over at her house. This held true regardless of where I was residing.

Sheila lived about fifteen minutes away in a small house set back out in the woods with her mother, stepfather, and sister. As children and teenagers, we loved running about through the woods at the back of her home.

The bathroom inside of her house had one long mirror with a sink at each opposite end, and the shower was enclosed in rock. As teenagers, we always had fun standing in her bathroom in front of that long mirror doing our hair and makeup.

We'd take a special delight in sneaking and watching R-rated movies together as teenagers and getting her cats drunk on hard liquor that we would always manage to procure from somewhere.

"Ok, who left the alcoholic eggnog on the countertop?" her sister, Tiffany, said one day as she came out of her bedroom, hands firmly placed on her hips.

Sheila and I looked at each other, barely hiding our amusement, both of us attempting to put on our best innocent faces.

"The cat got into it and is now back there throwing up," she exclaimed, even as she appeared to be slightly amused herself by the situation.

Sheila and I then rolled over onto the floor, laughing.

There were, I suppose, always two sides to me: growing up I was admittedly quite the tomboy. At the age of fifteen, I went to a local private school (the kind where you have to wear ugly plaid uniforms and stockings). I'd always leave my hair pulled back and rarely wore makeup.

One day the girls all gathered around me in the locker-room insisting on putting makeup on me. Despite my initial objections, the girls proceeded with the makeup.

"Does anyone have mascara?" one of the girls yelled out after they had layered my face with tons of eyeshadow and blush. Since nobody produced any mascara, they then just let it be and went about straightening my hair. After they finished, they all stepped back.

"Wow!" one of the girls exclaimed.

I looked in the mirror. The difference was indeed quite remarkable. I found that I liked this side of myself, this girlie side. I spent the rest of the day feeling quite confident in myself.

My school years were to be short-lived, however. I got in trouble in public school before I had transferred to private school. In an interview to be admitted to the private school, the headmaster, who was also the local church pastor, agreed to give me a chance at the school despite knowing that I had already encountered problems and had been in trouble in public school. I was admitted to the school even though my attendance there only lasted a year.

Everyone else at the school seemed to come from families who had more wealth and certainly lived in much nicer houses than me. I didn't always fit in well. I was also practically the only one who didn't play sports; not that there was much of an option in sports. You pretty much played basketball, and that was your only option. So, of course, everyone played basketball. Everyone that is, except me.

"Do you even go to this school?" a man asked me one day while I was sitting on the bleachers after I had informed him that I did not, in fact, play basketball.

11

He was joking, of course, but it did signify that I was a bit of an outcast. Eventually the coach of the girl's team- a short, stocky, manly type of woman- agreed to let me be the water girl for the team. It wasn't too bad of a gig. I didn't have to get sweaty, and I could at least travel with the team and fit in somehow.

Though I didn't play sports, I was still very aerobically fit and was always at a healthy weight. During physical fitness tests at school, I always performed very well aerobically, beating most of my other classmates whenever we would have to run track.

There was always one classmate, however, a boy named Kyle, who would always come out ahead of me. We ended up dating (if you can really call it "dating" at that age) for a few months, even though it was actually his younger brother Christian that I had a crush on.

I never did get the chance with Christian, however. At the age of sixteen, after my year in private school, I got my GED and left school completely.

I remember sitting in the headmaster's office of the private school I was attending. The headmaster did not want to sign off for me to get my GED.

"I don't feel like it's in your best interest," he said to me in an arrogant tone, refusing to sign off on the form. "I believe that God wants you to stay in school."

Lenard then went down to the public school for our jurisdiction and got the principal of that school to sign off on it.

It worked. I was able to pass the series of tests needed with the state and got the equivalent of a high-school diploma, all without ever officially finishing high school.

I only saw Christian one more time after that. He was involved in some drama with his possibly pregnant girlfriend, and I remember, upon seeing how his life had turned out, being glad that I had never gotten with him. Either way, I had long forgotten all about him once I left school.

After leaving school, I quickly move right into becoming independent. My first job was at a local small-town movie store. I also took a job on the side washing

dirty dishes in a local restaurant. I drove an old clunker
of a Cadillac around for my first car, but I didn't care. It
got me to where I wanted to go and allowed me the
freedom and independence to escape from life at home
and a way to escape from Lenard, who was always
finding something to be disagreeable about.

Sheila and I continued to hang out even though
she remained in high school. I was eventually able to get
Sheila a job at the same local movie store where I
worked. We had a lot of fun in those days. We would
both always hang out together at the movie store no
matter who was technically "on the clock." We'd play
around and view the merchandise to pass the time. We
also had a couple of other small jobs as teenagers that we
took together- such was the depth of our friendship.

Sheila had been dating Freddie on and off for
quite a long time. They appeared to me to be quite
compatible with each other in many ways. It was
remarkable how they appeared so alike, with both
having a somewhat rugged appearance and the same
color of hair and eyes. But I didn't really think much
about it. In either case, Sheila later dumped Freddie for

his cousin Jerry. That union produced six children, with the two officially marrying after child number three.

As for myself, I was always quite the picky one. Perhaps it was because I turned out to be quite on the extreme end of feminine in many ways, but there just weren't many guys out there that I found attractive. There were a couple, yet I still remained single. Despite all of my tomboy ways as a child and during my school years, the first desire of my heart was to get married and have children.

One evening right before closing time, Sheila and I were at the movie store together. We were all alone, except for one customer, a middle-aged woman, whom Sheila was checking out up at the counter (as she was the one who was technically on the clock that evening). A moment later two teenaged guys around our age walked through the door.

After the customer Sheila was checking out left, I then walked over to the counter. We observed the guys who had just walked in for a moment. The taller of the two guys was making some racket and talking loudly. We eventually walked over to talk to them.

"Hi," I said, introducing us. "I'm April. This is my friend Sheila."

"Hi," they both responded back in unison as they introduced themselves to us.

The taller one then spoke; "I'm Steven," he said. "This is my friend Dylan."

Sheila leaned over to whisper in my ear. "I like the shorter one; he's kind of hot."

"Ok, he's all yours," I told her. He was probably the better fit for her anyway, I reasoned as I observed his friend, who was still standing there smiling. He seemed more my type.

The guys continued to hang around until after we had closed the store. We all then made our way outside. Although nothing ever really developed between Sheila and Dylan, I found myself writing my number in Steven's checkbook before the night was over.

Two

$\mathcal{I}$t was only a couple of days before I received a phone

call from Steven. He was very charming. He asked me if
I wanted to go out that evening. I was excited. This was
the first time in my life that I had ever been about to
embark on anything real or even partially serious with a
member of the opposite sex. I agreed to go out with him,
and we made plans for a date. I then gave him directions
to my home.

Even though I was already out of school and
making my own money, I was only sixteen years old. At
this point in my life my mother had already moved away
from the lake house where my grandparents lived, and
the home I had stayed in with her. I moved back in with
Lenard even though I stayed gone as often as possible to

escape from his narcissistic and preaching ways. Due to his slovenly ways, I was also quite embarrassed to ever bring anyone over, save for the friends such as Sheila that I had grown up with.

Sitting out in the driveway, I was beginning to get a bit nervous. It was getting closer to 4:30. It wasn't long until I saw Steven's truck begin to pull up. I was excited. This was the first real date I had ever been on in my life. I had straightened out my hair and put on one of my favorite outfits- a pretty low-cut pink top and a pair of jean shorts.

I remember the moment when Steven got out of the truck. He was dressed real nice, and he smelled good. He was wearing a button-up shirt, with a white t-shirt on underneath and a pair of loose-fitting jeans. I never really liked the idea of tight jeans on a guy, it just always seemed a bit effeminate to me. He couldn't have been more perfect in my eyes.

When he got out, I noticed he held a single red rose in his hand. As he walked over to me, he held it out to me. I took it from him. I was elated. My heart soared. He talked to me for a minute before we left.

Right before we were about to leave, Lenard jumped into the passenger side of the truck with him and closed the door. It's not like I had to wonder what Lenard was saying to Steven. They were obviously talking about sex- as in *Don't do it.*

After we had left, I said to Steven, "So, what did he say to you?"

"He basically just said not to touch you," he replied with a smart-ass smile on his face.

Of course, it's not like that little talk would do a lot of good when all was said and done. Not that I ever did anything with Steven on the first date, or even the second one for that matter. In fact, it would take more work than Steven had probably ever imagined in his life just to even get that first kiss out of me.

Many years later he would go on to tell me "you had love in your eyes" when he would speak of that first date of ours. Of course, in the mind of a teenage boy, he had also confessed how he hoped that love would be transformed to lust.

He took me out to eat at an upscale burger joint which would become a historic landmark of sorts for our relationship even to this day. He ordered a hamburger and some fries. I ordered the same thing, much to the amusement of an elderly couple sitting across from us. I remember how he barely touched his food while I ate pretty much everything on my plate. I was never really one to turn down food.

He paid for everything and then we left to go to the movie theater. We talked for a minute about which movie we wished to see. I was hell-bent on seeing this ridiculous romantic comedy. He, however, suggested going to see the new *Dukes of Hazzard* movie.

"They got ol' Jessica Simpson playing Daisy Duke," he said, so I relented, and we went to see the *Dukes of Hazzard*.

At some point during the movie, he leaned over and said in my ear, "You can sit on my lap if you'd be more comfortable." I just giggled.

It was a bit chilly in the theater, and I shivered. Steven gave me his blue button-up over shirt to wear. I felt so comfortable and at ease with him. We turned our attention back to the movie, and he swore under his breath whenever Jessica Simpson came out in a bikini. Never being the jealous type, it didn't bother me any. Although I was still too naïve to understand parts of it, I had a good time and really got into the movie. The movie would go on to hold a very special place in my heart for years to come.

After that first date, we spent a lot more time together. There were several times we would hang out with Sheila and Freddie and have fun together. We pretty much did all of our hanging out over at Sheila's, as being at my place around Lenard was obviously not the optimal place for us all to be together. A week later Steven took me out to the movies again. This time I was gifted with a yellow rose from him.

One night after I was done working at the restaurant washing dishes, I came out to see Steven outside waiting for me. I had put my hair in a couple of braids and, as I always did after working in the restaurant, I smelled like grease and was just all around

21

filthy. It was truly one of the messiest jobs, with even my tennis shoes becoming soaked after only a couple loads of dishes.

I walked outside to see one of my co-workers, a larger girl a couple of years my senior, talking to Steven. I looked at him as if to say, "What's going on?" It was true that I felt a slight pang of jealousy at the situation this time around. After all, this wasn't just some virtual woman on the big screen but a real-life flesh and blood female. Steven said they had gone to school together. I supposed it wasn't that big of a deal, so I just brushed it off, never giving it another thought. Besides, as vain as it might have been, I was certain I was much prettier.

I then got into the truck with Steven and he took me to his house, despite my filthy state. Even though I felt icky, I would much rather have spent the time with Steven instead of going all the way home just to shower, so I dealt with it.

We walked in the door and his father, Cain, the man who was to one day become my father-in-law, was sitting off to the left in a chair at the computer. He was a good-looking man of about forty years of age. He was physically fit with dark hair and dark eyes. Of course, I was yet much too young to really notice any of that.

He was shirtless when we walked in but then politely put his shirt on after our arrival inside of the house. Steven introduced us, and we all sat and talked for a few minutes. I was very quiet and shy and didn't say much. Steven and I left a short time later.

Steven and I came back to his house a couple of times after that night whenever nobody else was around. We didn't do anything but talk, and I'd dance around a little bit with him to some music, and we'd hang out for a while.

Steven and I continued to hang out, with me even bringing him over to meet my mother one evening. We walked in through the door of the house, the very house where I had lived with her, my stepdad and two brothers growing up. She was sitting at the table in the kitchen, which was located to the left of the front door upon entering. She looked as though she was getting ready for bed, or perhaps had just simply been being lazy the whole day. She had no makeup on and seemed to be in an irritable mood.

Looking back, it probably wasn't the smartest move to introduce him to my mother so early, but I was really into him, and I was much too young to really know how to deal with guys. Steven seemed a bit uncomfortable with the situation, and my mother exclaimed how preoccupied she was.

"I would really only like to meet the guy you wish to get serious with," she said to me later. It was quite typical of my mother to bitch like that, so I just shrugged it off. In my mind, I was already contemplating getting serious with Steven. He seemed like the perfect guy and everything was going great.

Then all of a sudden one day Steven just disappeared.

Like pretty much every other teenage girl, I practically knew nothing about men or what the guys my age were thinking and the only "talk" I had ever received was from my mother, who just informed me about waiting to be "ready" for sex- whatever that was supposed to mean. Steven all of a sudden disappearing out of the blue on me was unexpected. I didn't know why it had happened or what I could have done about it. It was only many years later that I would realize that sex was the primary issue, as I hadn't had sex with him.

In reality, sex was never really on my mind, at least not to the point that I actually wanted to do it. Like most teenage girls, I had thought about it, but it was more-so just about discovering what it was all about and discovering my own sexual powers and how I could affect the guys around me. The women in the media acted sexually and we girls usually just strove to imitate them, even if we couldn't fully understand everything they were singing and talking about.

I found that Steven's disappearance bothered me. I found myself missing him. I tried to text him and call him a couple of times, but he never answered. I made some new friends around town in the area where he was from, and Sheila and I continued being friends as we had before. The only difference was that I suddenly found myself without a guy while she now had her choice of two different guys.

Distraught, I returned the two roses Steven had given me, which had already become dried out, and placed them, along with his shirt I had worn that day at the movie theater, in a box on his front doorstep. It was my way of saying good-bye.

Life went on and shortly after I turned seventeen I got a job answering the phone for a real estate company. I stayed at the job for nearly a year before they let me go. Even though answering phones was, in reality, quite easy, I was never really any good at the job. I also had to deal with the unmasked contempt of a female coworker who, in the hopes of getting rid of me, would go on to accuse me of flirting with every guy in the office. I guessed her to be somewhere in her mid-thirties. She was a habitual smoker with long bleach-blonde wavy hair. Being tall and skinny, she was still quite an attractive woman.

Her little schemes to get rid of me would eventually work for her. It wasn't even thirty seconds after I had been fired before she had already moved all of her items and taken over my old desk. *Oh well*, I thought, *it's really time to be moving on anyways*. I then went back to working more hours at the movie store again and hanging out with my friends.

Despite all the recent happenings in my life at that time, I could never quite get over Steven nor could I stop thinking about him. We ran into each other a few times at parties and a couple of the local hang-outs. He didn't interact with me all that much, while I would hang out in a crowd with other guys and a few girls-most of whom would only snub me. Though I had plenty of guys interested, including some that would be considered more "alpha," none of them ever really stood a chance with me. My heart was still all for Steven.

Out of the blue one evening, Steven called me. I agreed to come hang out with him. I headed to his house, but when I got up to the driveway, I was confused. The trailer he was living in when he brought me over the last time was gone. There was nothing there but a blank lot where the trailer-house had been.

Thoroughly confused, I called Steven. "What happened to the house? Where am I supposed to go?" I asked.

"It's the house down the hill," he informed me.

"Ok. I'll be there in a minute." I said and hung up.

I came down to the house and knocked on the door. The house wasn't very big, but it was nice and obviously new. The sun had already set so I couldn't make out many details about the outside of the house. Steven answered the door a minute later. He was all alone.

"Where's your dad?" I asked him. The house was so quiet.

"He's visiting his girlfriend," he said.

He let me in the house, and we sat down on the couch together. He had a 30-pack of beer at his feet and asked me if I wanted one. I declined. I was much too nervous and didn't really feel like drinking. We sat for a few minutes making small talk before he casually draped his arm over the sofa behind me.

It wasn't too long before he made his move. I was really into him, so I agreed to go to his room with him. After all, we were all alone, and he was the one that I wanted.

When we got into his bedroom, I let him undress me. He fumbled for a minute with my bra before he figured out that it had to be undone from the front. He made a slight comment on it, and I slightly laughed and blushed a little. Then I went to bed with him.

I'm not sure exactly what I was expecting. It was my first time doing anything like that. Sure, I had kissed a couple of guys in the past, but it had never really gone further than that. None of them ever really did it for me the way Steven did. I had never really liked any other guy enough to even consider the possibility of sex.

The sex didn't last long, only a couple of minutes. Was there supposed to be more? I didn't know, but I was with Steven and I was happy. He was all I wanted, and if sex allowed me to be with him then so be it. We were still alone in the house, so I stayed with him all of that night- our first night together.

Three

$\mathcal{T}$he next morning I opened my eyes to see the sun

coming in through the window behind me. So, this wasn't a dream. I was really here, in Steven's bed. I looked over at him. He was still asleep.

Figuring I looked quite a mess, I got up quietly and tiptoed into the bathroom next door to freshen up my face and try to straighten out my hair some. I then came back into the room just as Steven was waking up.

"Good morning," he said to me with a pleased smile on his face.

I smiled back. "Good morning," I quietly replied back to him. I still hadn't gotten over my internal shyness, and I was particularly shy at that moment, given what we had shared the previous evening.

I wasn't sure what move to make next. Steven got up out of bed, and we walked together into the living room. I had worn his shirt the night before as I hadn't planned on staying and certainly didn't pack any kind of bag for the occasion. It was a decorative white hunting t-shirt and before I left he told me I could keep it. I remember how I cherished that t-shirt for a long time to come, often sleeping in it even when I was at home alone and hadn't seen Steven for a long time.

He had this smile on his face. If I had perhaps been just a bit wiser or just a bit older, I might have easily seen right through his façade. Little did I know that he had no intentions of being real with me after I left that morning. Little did I know that I had just been played. I was yet only seventeen years old and still so very ignorant to the ways of the world- and in particular the ways of men.

A few minutes later we said our goodbyes and I got into my truck to leave. It was still early, and I was very sleepy- but also very happy. Ignorance is bliss, as they say. Indeed, it truly is.

I don't know what I was expecting from Steven (a
relationship maybe? a single phone call at least?), but it
was a while before I heard from him again. Whenever I
wasn't working, I would spend my time hanging out
with friends. Sheila was preoccupied those days with
baby number one that she just had with Jerry, so I spent
more time hanging out with another friend that I had
gone to school with, Sally.

Sally was a short girl who was a bit "chunky."
She had medium-length blonde hair and a bad
complexion. She was one of the few "approved" friends,
other than Sheila, that I ever brought over to Lenard's.
She officially lived with her mother, yet spent the
weekends with her father. Maybe only once did Sally
and I ever hang out over at her mother's. We were
always over at her father's. The one and only time we
ever hung out over at her mother's we spent the evening
watching one of the *Exorcist* movies. I would then go on
to have nightmares for approximately the next five

years. That's about the point when I decided I was more of a romantic-comedy type of girl.

Sally's father was a chain-smoker who spent his evenings sitting in front of the TV lighting up one right after the other. Ironically, he wasn't overweight, and I don't believe he even suffered from any health problems. Both of Sally's parents were quite old, appearing to be senior citizens already, which I always found quite odd, given the ages of Sally and I.

When we were a bit younger, Sally and I would have fun going through her dad's not-so-secret Playboy stash. We knew he kept them hidden away in his closet, so whenever he would leave the house for a while, we'd go exploring.

"In here!" Sally would say as she dug through the closet.

"Hurry!" I would hiss at her a few minutes later upon hearing the front door open and close.

We would then rush around, trying to shove all the magazines up high in the closet where she had gotten them from before we got caught. We'd then run out of the room as fast as we could to the safety of Sally's bedroom and pray we'd been quick enough.

Through my friend Sally, I would then go on to be introduced to mutual friend Chelsea. Chelsea was a daughter to a single mother and had several other siblings as well- some residing in the home and some not.

Chelsea was a pretty girl with a nice figure. She had what I would term to be a "horse-face," however. Despite living entirely different lifestyles, the two of us soon became best friends. From there on I was always over at her house, or she was always over at mine. We went practically everywhere together and were rarely apart. It would only be later on, when she and I both became mothers, that we would finally go our separate ways. At that point in my life, the differences between our two lifestyles were simply too much to ignore, so I cut her out of my life entirely and had no further contact with her.

Chelsea lived close in the same area where Steven was from, and I found myself coming into contact with Steven more often. We would often go to parties where Steven would be as well. There were several times when Steven would call me up, and we would hang out together, though his phone calls were not always consistent. Sometimes he would take me fishing or we would hang out with a couple of other friends of his at the lake. I considered those times with Steven to be pleasant. There were many other times, however, when Steven would ring up my phone at night whenever he was drunk.

On one particular night, I was visiting with my mother in her new home. She had just recently moved and was now about a forty-five-minute drive away, which meant I could still visit her often. I had rented some movies from the movie store by my mother's house. It was a much bigger and nicer store than the small one that I still worked in back in my hometown.

Only about a quarter of the way through the movie, my phone began to go off several times. It was Steven. I just ignored it. He and his friend Christopher were drunk again. They began leaving messages on my phone, being complete assholes and calling me names, telling me how awful and ugly I was.

"Listen to the way he's talking to you!" my mother said to me upon hearing the messages.

"I know," I replied.

Did Steven's behavior bother me? Yes, perhaps a little, but I wasn't one to get very easily offended. I laughed it off. It didn't make me want him any more or any less. I liked Steven a lot, and I guess in my teenage mind I reasoned that if I just put up with his behavior long enough or perhaps even pursued him a little more and gave him all the sex he wanted then somehow we'd end up living happily-ever-after in fairytale land.

Boy was I ever wrong. I would meet Steven up whenever he called me, and I was always there for him. But was he ever around when I wanted or needed him? Of course not. It was a one-sided "relationship"- if a relationship is what you could even call it.

I don't know what it was I saw in Steven. I guess all my life I had simply been looking for a home and a family, and I knew Steven came from probably one of the biggest families around. As I had always been an outcast, I so desperately wanted a home and a family that I could call my own. Therefore Steven became the one I wanted for just that purpose. No other guy would do for me.

The interactions between Steven and I were not all one-sided. Though I did chase Steven by calling him and texting him and doing all I could to be around him and to be where he was, he did more than his fair share of calling me up as well.

One fall evening a few months before my eighteenth birthday there was a big party going on at an old hunting place that everyone knew about. As was sometimes typical, Steven was there.

I had come to the party with my friend Caitlyn. Caitlyn wasn't ever a real good friend of mine, but we did hang out quite a bit as teenagers. We at least got along well with each other. Caitlyn wasn't exactly what one would consider to be traditionally pretty. She wore glasses and was a bit overweight, with most of the weight being centered around her gut. In fact, the first time I met her, I actually wondered if she was expecting a child. She wasn't, of course. She was just simply fat.

Caitlyn lived in a very nice home inside a gated community with her mother. She claimed to have an older sister who she swore had a criminal record a mile long from prostitution. The friendship between Caitlyn and I lasted for a couple of years until we parted ways and never spoke to each other again after she moved away and I began my own family.

That night at the party, Steven chatted up my friend Caitlyn and ultimately ended up taking her home with him. Bright and early the next morning my phone started going off.

"How did I end up going home with her?" It was Steven. He had finally sobered up and didn't seem too very pleased with himself. I, however, was quite happy. I saw my opportunity for a bit of revenge when he then proceeded to ask, "Can you come pick her up for me?"

"You are the one who took her home with you! You got yourself into this situation; now you can just kindly get yourself right back out of it." I then hung up the phone.

Though I loved Steven, that was just going way too far. He had left me at the party that night crying. Not only the fact that he took my friend home with him- the very friend I had come to the party with nonetheless- but also the fact that she agreed to go with him did not escape me.

That night after they left, I was standing off to the side by the tree-line crying. Upon hearing footsteps behind me, I turned around. A local boy a bit older than myself came up behind me to talk to me.

Putting his hands in his pockets, he said to me, "Why aren't you mad at him instead of crying over him? What kind of friend is she that she would go home with the guy you like and betray you like that?"

I just shook my head and said: "I know." The tears continued to fall down my face as I spoke with him. I still couldn't help but love Steven, I told him.

Understanding then seemed to dawn in his eyes. "He took your virginity, didn't he?" he asked me.

I just looked at him, slightly nodding but never really answering either way. Of course, that made sense. I had given Steven my body. He had been the first and only one I had been with, and I still didn't really want anyone else. Of course, I wasn't stupid. I knew the guy talking to me was probably hoping to pick me up himself. But it still felt good to have someone to talk to about the situation.

As odd as it may seem to the casual observer, I continued to be friends as usual with Caitlyn. I made Steven deal with the mess he had created and brought upon himself, and that very afternoon I was back hanging out with Caitlyn as if nothing ever happened. Even to this very day, I'm not clear on whether or not anything actually did happen between them. Steven was so drunk, apparently, that even to this very day he doesn't remember anything about it. Of course, that's not so unusual. He would later go on to claim that he never remembered very much at all about those days when we were younger. He apparently developed an alcohol problem and stayed drunk all of the time.

Later on, years after our marriage, he confessed that I was part of the reason he stayed drunk. He just couldn't get me off of his mind. In the typical fashion of most teenage boys, however, the word "commitment" was the scariest word on the planet to him, and something to be avoided at all costs.

So it happened a couple of days later that I was driving along near sundown. I was admittedly a bit of an airhead in those days and was running low on gas. No, I wasn't running low on gas. *Damn it*, I thought. I was *out* of gas.

Though I don't understand why, it was Cain that I ended up calling. To this day I don't even know how it was that I came to have his number, nor can I comprehend how it is that I can still remember it even to this very day. He came and put gas in my truck for me. It was already after dark. He didn't say much and I thanked him.

I was still so young at that time, yet somehow something was beginning inside of me. He had planted something inside of my mind that would stay with me as I matured over the years. Many years later, he would become something very meaningful to me, although I couldn't know it yet.

Four

"Here's to my first legal cigarette," I said as I flicked

my thumb across the end of the lighter and lit the end of
the cigarette I was holding in my hand.

Isabella laughed beside me, and I did the same
thing. It was my eighteenth birthday today. What this
also meant to me was that Lenard could never do
anything to ever control me again.

My mother felt quite the same way. My coming
of age was, as she had so gleefully told me many times,
"…the last time I will ever have anything to do with
your father ever again."

My friendship with Isabella was quite a short-
lived one. We had met through a mutual friend, or
perhaps I should say acquaintance, of ours, and we only

hung out a few times before we parted ways never to see each other again.

That evening I went out to a local strip-club. *I can do this for some good cash*, I thought.

When I entered into the bar, I proceeded to tell them I wanted a job. They put me to work immediately. It was a small bar, a real dive if you want to get technical about it. Compared to what one might typically expect to make in that profession, the money wasn't all that great, but it sure beat any other job I could find in such a small town. All of my other options were quite bleak.

Though I could have easily made ten times the money in a bigger city, I brought in enough cash to live easy and was always able to go on shopping sprees and take my friends out anywhere we all wanted to go. It also freed me up from any job obligations during the day so I could hang out with friends- and I was always hanging out with someone, as I found going home to be a very lonely experience.

My social awkwardness carried on with me even well into my adult years. Though most of the girls would have their "regular" customers come in that would be faithful with spending copious amounts of money on them, I never had that. Of course, I did always wonder if my keeping "clean" was part of the reason why. Though I had no problem showing off the goods, I was never content with any man ever trying to touch me, and I certainly never consented to do anything more than dance- no matter the price. It just wasn't in me. I was still a "good girl" in a lot of ways, but I never saw anything shameful in showing off my body. It was just dancing, and I made good money without ever having to compromise myself.

Though I never had any regular customers of my own, there were a couple of gentlemen that frequented the club who always bought me drinks (which I got paid for) and ordered dances from me. One of them was an elderly gentleman. He would always sit at the bar and buy me drinks and randomly place tips in my thong. He was always very polite and distinguished every time he would interact with me, so it was to my surprise a couple of months later when he tried to stick his hands down my pants during the first lap dance he had ever bought from me.

He paid good money for the dance, as it was a rather lengthy one. When he attempted to touch me, however, I backed away from him, gently shaking my head "no."

"I thought I could do that in here," he said to me.

"I'm sorry," I told him. "I don't…"

He was a great customer, and I enjoyed his company, so I hated what I had to say to him, but no amount of money was worth allowing him to do *that* to me. He didn't push any further, and I finished out the dance.

After that night I thought for sure that would be the last time I would ever receive a drink from him. To my astonishment, however, he continued buying me drinks and carrying on polite conversation with me every time he would come in- he just never bought another lap dance from me again.

Though I did smoke cigarettes for a time, quitting after a few short months upon becoming pregnant, I never did any type of drugs. Quite frankly, the very idea of drugs had scared me ever since somebody had convinced me to try some marijuana at a party one time. I ended up smoking way too much and being in a state of paranoia for the next two hours (perhaps it was more than marijuana in that joint?)

It was Diana, of course, who offered up that joint to me that night at the party. The party was located in the same location where we had all been at that night when Steven took Caitlyn home with him. Of course, it's not like there were all that many party spots in the area, especially for teenagers. We pretty much just grabbed whatever available location in the woods we could find where we could drive a few four-wheel drives into and park them all around a campfire. That was our idea of a "party" in those days.

My friend Diana was a rough sort of woman. She lived on this little plot of land in a camper with her Native-American boyfriend. She referred to him as her "fiancé," even though the pair would go on to break up only six months later. It was her idea, of course, as he would have done anything to get her back. He even showed up outside the movie store one night when I was closing up, asking if I had seen her and asking me if I could talk to her for him. He was crazy over her.

In the end, just like with Chelsea, lifestyle differences got in the way of mine and Diana's friendship, and I cut things off with her. Being that she had, by that point, already moved about an hour away to live with her mother, our friendship had pretty much already faded out.

It was only a couple of months after I began to strip full-time that racetrack season came around. All of a sudden the bar was filled with the jockeys and workers from the racetrack. I quickly made friends with many of them, and they invited me back to the back where the workers were. They even offered to let me ride the horses on occasion. It had been so long since I had been on a horse.

"Would you like to ride a pony?" Pedro said to me one day as he walked out of the stables.

"Sure!" I told him as images of a cute little Shetland type of pony floated through my head. He then disappeared into the stables again only to return a moment later with the biggest horse I had ever seen in my entire life.

"That's a pony?" I asked him incredulously.

"You said you wanted to ride a pony." He replied, looking mischievous.

"That horse is huge!" I replied as my eyes opened up wider than I had ever thought possible. I took a few deep breaths to try and steady my nerves, figuring there was no hope of backing out now without looking like a coward.

"Ok, I'm ready," I said after a minute. I walked over to the horse, and Pedro helped me up into the saddle then handed me the reins.

I was still inside of the stables at this point, as I hadn't thought to lead the horse out before I mounted him. Laughing nervously I asked, "How do I get him out of here?"

The horse was so tall I thought my head might get taken off if I tried to walk him out while still atop him. The horse itself was nearly as tall as the stables!

Pedro chuckled as he took the reins from me. He then began leading the horse out of the stables for me. I ducked and closed my eyes until I was sure that all was clear. A small crowd had begun to gather at this point.

Ok, I'm seriously ready to get off of this 'pony,' the biggest horse I've ever seen in my life! I thought. However, being as how I had already drawn so much attention to myself, I had no real choice other than to take the reins and slowly- very slowly- ride the horse around for a few minutes.

After a couple of times around the barn, I promptly dismounted. I was still shaking a bit. Although I had always enjoyed riding horses, my fear of heights did make me a bit paranoid at times due to how far off the ground I often sat when riding. But I had made it. I had survived. I then silently vowed to myself that I would never ask to ride a "pony" around there ever again.

I did have some good times working as an "exotic dancer," if you will. But it wasn't all bliss by any means. Many of the other girls would become mean and catty. This behavior is common in women anyway, but a business where women are all competing for men every night based on their looks just magnifies it about a hundred-fold. I was very young and had not quite developed my personality and self-confidence to the point of being able to deal with it effectively. I was also very naïve, which did ironically make it easier to dance for the men every night, grinding on their laps and taking their money. Later on, however, I would discover just how hard it would be to keep up that lifestyle once that innocence was shattered.

It had been a while since I had seen or heard from Steven and a couple of guys from the racetrack had commanded my attention. I even began to develop some feelings for one of them, a guy named Andrew.

Andrew was tall, probably around five-foot-eleven or so- about as tall as Steven was. He had blonde hair that he kept down to his shoulders. Normally I didn't like the hippy look on guys, but it seemed to fit him well. I would jokingly call him "Harry," and he liked it. We hung out a few times, though nothing ever got real serious. Nothing ever progressed past the point of making out, anyway. I would never consent to go "all the way" with him, or any other guy for that matter, as my heart was still with Steven. In fact, I was given the nickname "The Tease" by all the guys, as I would smile coyly and flirt, but never grant sexual access to any of them.

I agreed to take a trip out of state whenever Andrew and the rest of the crew left the local racetrack to travel to the next place they were working. My heart was still somewhat torn apart from Steven being gone for so long, and I thought getting away might be good for me and help get my mind off of him. I would look at my phone, knowing it was unlikely he would ever call. It had been at least three months since I had last heard from him. I wasn't even sure what I felt anymore for him. I was beginning to get tired of dealing with him. I was so exhausted from all the games he played and all of his ways.

The night before Andrew was to leave, I quit work early. I was getting a bit emotional over him as I had grown a bit attached to him over the time that he'd been there. We were sitting up at the bar together. I hadn't really been doing my job all night and had made very little money. I had been ignoring other potential customers to spend the short amount of time I had left with Andrew. He was leaving, and I wanted to go with him. Upon talking with the manager, she agreed to cut my pay in half, but I didn't care.

"I'll half your pay," Irina said from behind the bar.

"Ok," I said as I held back my tears. I immediately left to go to the dressing room to gather my things.

"Are you leaving?" one of the friendlier girls asked me.

"Yeah, I don't really feel like staying here anymore tonight. I'm not feeling real well."

She looked as though she understood. "Good luck," she said.

"Thanks." I smiled at her and continued to pack my things. They could keep it all for all I cared. I was going with Andrew.

I stayed with Andrew back at the stables for quite a while that night as he gave me the address to where he would be.

"I'll see you there," he said as he planted a kiss on my forehead. I then turned to leave.

I went back home and packed my things and tried to get some sleep. The next morning I got in my truck and headed out of town to travel three states away to where Andrew was going to be.

Five

$\mathcal{I}$ did have quite a bit of fun on my journey out of state to see and be with Andrew. I traveled to places I had never been before in my life. I ate in new restaurants, shopped in new malls. I had enough cash with me and in the bank to live for at least a good solid month before I would ever have to worry about going back to work. Besides, I was sure there would be a good strip club somewhere where I could strip for a night or two if I got into a pinch.

I stopped at every state to stay the night in a hotel to allow me plenty of time as I was traveling though. I finally arrived at the track where Andrew was working and staying three days later. Upon arriving, I was given a place to stay by one of the ex-managers of the club I worked. She had up and had an epiphany one night all of a sudden- or something- where she left the club and never came back.

I remember that night, of course. She threw up her hands saying how she was fed up with everyone and everything at the club. She then cussed out everyone, customers included, hopped in her truck and sped out of state to cohabit with her boyfriend. She then became an official member of the track. She allowed me to stay in her room as she was staying with her boyfriend.

It wasn't long, however, before issues cropped up between us. I wanted to spend my time going to the lake with the friends I had made. I didn't care about learning the tools of the trade (shoeing horses and things like that) the way she wanted me to. She was not happy about it, of course, and refused to have anything more to do with me.

Whatever, I thought. I hadn't spent a bunch of time with Andrew since I had been there anyway. Whatever I had initially felt for him was beginning to fade away. Hardly even saying a word, I packed my things and left.

I took my time coming back home, stopping and staying in every state along the way the same as I had on my journey there. But this time things seemed a bit different. While I did feel a greater sense of peace inside of me, there was still this sense of sadness in my heart. It was almost like there was this impending doom beating down on me and as I got closer to home, all of the feelings I had pushed away regarding Steven were slowly coming back.

I settled back into life at home the way I had before, only this time without all of my racetrack friends. I knew they'd be back again in a few months, however, whenever the season started back up again. In the meantime, I just continued on with life as normal. I hadn't seen Steven around at any parties lately. Of the very few that I had been to, he hadn't been there. I don't know why that was exactly.

It wasn't until one day when I was standing around in a deserted parking lot with a small group of people that all of a sudden Steven drove up. He didn't pull in to where we were but just simply stopped his truck and rolled down the window.

Looking over to where I was standing, he gave me a wink and smiled, saying, "How you doin'?"

The nerve of him! I hadn't heard from him for months, and all of a sudden he thought he could just waltz right into our little circle like nothing had ever happened? Like he'd caused absolutely no hurt or pain to me or anyone else by his absence? I had never been more insulted in my life.

I don't know what I was thinking, but I was determined. I walked straight towards where he sat so arrogantly and comfortably in that truck of his, raised up my hand and gave him a good smack right across the face. He obviously wasn't expecting that one! All of a sudden that smug smile was gone off of his face, and he drove off as fast as he could.

Kevin, one of the local boys, was behind his truck at that exact moment relieving himself. He came out, exclaiming, "What the hell? I was back there pissin' when I heard this 'smack.' I was like, telling it to hurry up and trying to peer around the back of my truck to see what was going on!"

Ok, he's clearly already had one too many, I thought.

Kevin was an interesting sort of guy. I never really liked him all that much but I never really disliked him either. From my point of view, he just simply existed. He was, however, a very good looking guy- that much I could never deny. Standing just over six feet tall, he was tall and well-built.

Though I never did get with him in any way, he took it upon himself after he had a few too many drinks one night to hop in the truck with me as I was getting ready to leave one of our little backwoods parties. He already had a girlfriend and was also screwing around with some other girl on the side.

"What do you want?" I asked him that night.

"Why do you still take an interest in Steven?" he asked me. "What does he have that he could offer you? The guy doesn't even have any heat in his house or anything! He's a complete bum!"

"I don't think that's really any of your business, is it?" I semi-yelled at him. He then began to get that look in his eyes. *Uh-oh*, I thought. He reached over and grabbed me, attempting to shove his tongue down my throat.

"Quit!" I exclaimed as I pushed him off of me. He backed off. He appeared pissed, though. He abruptly got out of my truck, slammed the door, and stalked away.

It wasn't long before I had to contend with Kevin's real bitch of a girlfriend. The girl was nearly as tall as he was. I thought her and Kevin to be very well matched together. Being a bitch wasn't just an attitude with her- it was a lifestyle. The next time I came up to a party, she jumped me...

"I'm telling you, don't go to that party," the girl who had really been fooling around with Kevin told me a few hours before the party that evening. "She's been telling everyone in town that the next time she sees you she's going to kick your ass."

"She's full of shit," I replied.

"I'm telling you just don't go."

"I'm going anyways. Screw her. I haven't done anything with her precious boyfriend. It was him who came and stuck his goddamned tongue down my throat! Let her try something."

Fully believing her not to be serious, I went to the party. She was the center of attention that night, standing around the campfire. There were about fifteen others or so present.

She didn't waste any time after I had arrived before she began calling me about every name in the book. She then came up and grabbed my hair and yanked as hard as she could and started hitting me.

She was nearly twice my size, this Amazon Woman, and she quickly knocked me to the ground. I couldn't keep up with her or fight her off. A few minutes later, a couple of others jumped in to try and pull her off of me, eventually succeeding.

It was just an all around crappy night for me. Before even getting to the party that evening I had already had to fight off one asshole who insisted I go down on him if I wanted to ride any further with him. I had earlier agreed to ride along to the store with him for some drinks. He then turned into the biggest jerk I had ever run across in my life. He was so rude. Already halfway to the store, he basically told me to either put out or get out.

I looked over at him, disbelieving, and said, "Are you serious?" He insisted he was."Fine, I'll walk," I said.

I then got out of his truck and slammed the door. I headed back to the party, walking in the pitch dark, to get back just in time to be assaulted by Amazon Woman.

I was very shaken up by the events of the night and headed back home, admittedly with a few tears in my eyes. On the way home the girl who had been screwing around on the side with Kevin called me up, pleading for me not to say anything about it. I promised not to say anything. At least she had warned me earlier that day about Amazon Woman's intentions to do me in at the party.

"Whatever," I said, hanging up the phone. I then proceeded to wish them all a crappy life and went home.

It was a nice sunny Saturday afternoon a couple of weeks later when my phone started going off. It was Steven, asking me to come over.

By this point, however, I was already so exhausted from dealing with him. I was exhausted with his disappearing and reappearing out of my life. I was tired of his asshole ways and was almost to the point of just completely giving up on him. But in the back of my mind, I still had these dreams and visions of a happy home and family- a home and family I still thought he might be able to give me. Still believing there to be some chance for it, I consented to come over to his house.

I pulled up to his house, and he let me in. It was sometime around noon. We came up to the top floor of his house and hung out for a few minutes. He made small talk with me for a minute or two. Being the naturally quiet and shy type of person that I am, I didn't say a whole lot but just meekly replied a little bit whenever he'd say something to me. I then let him have sex with me, as usual.

I was very confused by the sex this time. It only seemed to last less than a minute before he looked up at me strangely and pulled out of me.

Afterward, I went to the bathroom to pee and noticed something white and thick draining out of me. Being the naïve eighteen-year-old that I was, I was confused as to what was going on. Looking back on the situation later, I understood that he had ejaculated into me. The look on his face as he looked up at me was clearly the result of him having realized what he'd done.

He wasn't wearing a condom. Indeed, rarely did he ever wear one anytime we were together. I hadn't taken any birth control pills since I was fifteen, when my mother took me to get a physical and let me get on the pill. The prescription was simply allowed to expire as I got older and, being that I eventually wanted to have a family, I never really bothered with it after that.

A few minutes later, Steven's younger brother Joey drove by Steven's house with his friends. Joey then called up Steven wondering what he had been doing with me. I was a bit preoccupied and didn't catch what

Steven's reply was. I thought he had just simply hung up the phone.

A week later Steven and I were together again, driving down a dirt road alone with each other in the middle of the night. He turned on some music as the landscape flashed by us out the windows. He then conceived the brilliant idea that I should get on top of him and ride him as we were going down the road. I agreed to do what he wanted and hopped in the driver's seat on top of him while he was still driving. Looking back, I'll never know how we didn't crash. He kept on driving as everything whirled around us in a blur and faded away.

Despite all of the times that we had sex, it's not like he ever made me orgasm. I didn't even know for sure what an orgasm was. I just liked being in his company. That was all that mattered to me, and that was more fun than anything else. He got the sex and I got his time and attention. For now anyway…

About three weeks later I was at work sitting at the bar talking to a co-worker, an older woman, who managed the place sometimes. We were heavily involved in conversation regarding the recent happenings in our lives. I told her I had been very tired recently and had a drastic change in appetite.

"When was the last time you had your period?" she asked.

"About five weeks ago, I guess" I replied.

"Five weeks!?" she repeated.

"Yeah."

"I'm telling you; you've got to be pregnant," she said.

"I don't think so," I said.

"Just get a test and see."

"Ok," I finally relented.

I somewhat hoped inside that it could be true. If I was indeed pregnant, then I would finally, after all that time, have something that would tie me to Steven. My intentions towards him were never bad, however. I just wanted to be with him, and to have a family with him would have been the greatest thing in the world to me. I wanted nothing else from him but his love.

Walking into a local drug store, I picked up a couple of reliable looking tests off of the shelf. What those tests would end up telling me would go on to change my life forever- in both the best and the worst ways.

Six

$\mathcal{I}$ didn't want to take those tests alone, so I called up

a friend of mine, Zoe, who I had been hanging out with a bit at that time in my life. We sat in her bathroom together while I took both of them. They were both positive. I was glad that Zoe was with me at that time as I really needed a second party to confirm what I thought my eyes were seeing.

Zoe was actually a very pretty girl who was exactly my own age. It's amazing that she turned out as well as she did, in my opinion, given the family that she came from.

The entire time we were there at Zoe's house, her mother would continuously pound on the door to her room and the door to her bathroom.

"What are you doing in there?" she yelled at us.

"Nothing!" Zoe yelled back at her mother.

Being that the tests were showing positive, my first priority at that time was to simply get out of there in order to protect the growing life inside of me. I told Zoe I would see her later and she walked me out to my truck as I just barely escaped her mother's wrath.

Though I would continue to hang out with Zoe many times after that day, and even catch up with her years later to rekindle our friendship, I never came back to her mother's house again. Zoe eventually ended up moving away a short time later after her mother was relocated to a "home."

I went home and told both my mother (over the phone), and then Lenard that I was going to have a baby. Of course, I was already eighteen years old and technically an adult, but I was happy about the baby and still unsure of what I was supposed to do. Both repeated the same thing to me.

"Don't tell him!" they each exclaimed whenever I told them the news.

But what kind of a life was that? Would I have ever put myself in a position to be having a baby with him in the first place if I didn't actually want to be with him in the long-term? What was the purpose of anything if I could not be with him? I couldn't do what it was they wanted me to do. I picked up the phone and called Steven.

This time he answered. "Hello," he said.

"I need to talk to you," I told him.

"You're not pregnant, are you?" he said in a cocky tone. I then hung up the phone.

I didn't hang up the phone for any reason other than pure nerves. I couldn't bring myself to actually tell him "yes." Looking back, perhaps I should have never called him for that purpose. Perhaps it would have been better to have confronted him in person instead of just phoning. Perhaps if I had, things would have worked out differently. But *should* things have worked out differently? Would I have gone on to be the person that I am today if things hadn't happened the way that they did?

Perhaps if he had not done to me all of the things that he was fixing to do, my life would have been worse. Perhaps we would have had even more problems and hardships than what we ultimately went on to have. Perhaps I would have had even more children with him and messed up my life even worse. Only God can truly know the answer to that one.

Steven never called me back after that. He instead called a mutual friend, or should I say an acquaintance of ours, Mia, to ask her to snoop around for him and find out if I was indeed pregnant. Mia then called me up asking about it. I came over to her place to take another test- which also came out positive, of course. Mia then reported back to Steven that, yes, I was indeed pregnant.

Mia and I ended up developing a friendship after that day; a friendship which would end up being critical to my survival in the days following the birth of my baby. I'm not sure what I had truly expected from Steven, but he just seemed to go crazy. Like a lot of guys his age, he didn't want to admit to what he had done nor take any responsibility for his actions. He denied all responsibility for getting me pregnant and instead dropped off the face of the earth, claiming to anyone that would listen to him that the child was not his. Yet even though he kept defaming my name at every chance he got, I still loved him and hoped to get with him.

I knew that I had to do something different with my life at this point. I was still living with Lenard, and there was no way I was about to bring a baby into the world living there in that house with him. No way. I needed privacy, and I needed space.

As interesting as it might seem, I kept my job as an exotic dancer all throughout my pregnancy, up until the very day that I gave birth, and I used the money I got from stripping to rent my own three bedroom, two bathroom home. I called Lenard up as soon as I had made my preparations and told him I was moving out. Once I had gone, I never moved back in again.

I felt the feminine energy inside of me and dreamed of having an all-natural birth in the privacy of my home. I didn't want to miss a thing about being female- and I didn't.

I was healthy and young, and everything was going well for me. I made the appointments with my midwife. It was just me, her and her apprentice who was always there. As well, they were the only ones present the day when my baby would be delivered. My midwife understood completely when I said that I did not want anyone to be informed whenever I went into labor. It was a common request, and one she respectfully honored. I would go on to have a healthy baby girl- whom I would name Hope, as hope is what she had given me- with no injuries, no complications, and no need for medicine on one beautiful evening a few months down the road.

Sometime when I was about six months along, on a Friday night, I had the most pleasant of surprises. It was a crowded night, and I was working the floor (as they had quit allowing me on the stage a couple of weeks back), when I looked up and saw Christopher come through the door with Steven in tow right behind him.

It was apparently Christopher's birthday, and they were there to celebrate. All other thoughts fled my mind whenever I laid eyes upon Steven. They took a table towards the back of the room. I came over and sat with them. Steven motioned me over to come and sit on his lap. There were some men behind me that kept trying to grab at me, but I swatted them away. I was all for Steven that night. We talked for a little bit then Steven got up for a minute to visit the restroom.

While he was gone, Christopher leaned over and said to me, "That's his baby, he needs to be taking care of you. You shouldn't be left alone here in this mess."

With pain in my eyes, I looked down and said: "I know."

When Steven returned, Christopher handed him money to go and get a lap-dance from me. Steven took the money he had been given and paid for the dance. Afterward, I led him off into the private room located behind the bar. I jumped on his lap and started grinding on him. I then stopped and kissed him. It seemed like I was doing something naughty and forbidden at that moment. I knew a lot of the other girls had no problem doing sexual "favors" for the guys, but I had never been one of them- until this moment. It was like it was when we were younger, when we first met, when I would giggle whenever he would take me out on a date.

But I knew this moment would not last forever. Soon he would be gone, leaving me all alone here at the club- leaving me all alone in life. I would be going home alone. Even though I had friends such as Mia and Chelsea that I hung out with, it wasn't the same. There was also Nathan, a guy who showed an acute interest in wanting to be with me, but I never could return his love.

Nathan was a good guy. He was a true country boy, living back out in the woods with his folks still. He would later go on to marry someone else and move away. He was tall and dark and a bit on the hefty side. I wouldn't have described him as exceptionally handsome, but he wasn't all that bad. We would hang out a lot as if we were some kind of unofficial couple, but I never granted him more than a mere kiss the whole time he was in my company. He was a friend to me, nothing more. Perhaps one day there could have been something more, but at this time I just wasn't feeling it.

He and Steven would go on to fight over me after Hope was born. Steven was sitting in the living room one night while Nathan was standing by the door. There was a silent exchange that went on between the two guys that night. The tension was thick in the air.

"I'll see you later," Nathan told me before stalking out the front door of my home. Steven remained on the couch looking satisfied as if he had just run off his rival.

A week later I found myself sitting in the passenger seat of Nathan's truck. Not much was said between us.

"I'm sorry. He's the father of my child," I told him as I quietly opened the door and slipped away.

Nathan then went over a couple of houses down to a mutual friend of ours. With a heavy heart, he reportedly said "She chose him," before he walked out the door and out of all of our lives for good.

As far as Steven was concerned, I was starting to have my own misgivings about him after Hope was born. *What have I done?* I thought silently to myself.

I felt as if I had just ruined my entire life, as if I had just foolishly thrown away my future. What had Steven contributed up to this point? What had he ever done but call me names, tell lies about me and deny his responsibilities? I had taken on all of the blame, all of the responsibility while he had contributed absolutely nothing but thirty seconds of his time on a pretty Saturday afternoon.

But what was I to do now? The birth of our child had irrevocably tied me to him for the rest of our lives. He already knew about the child's existence. The only thing that I could realistically do now was to try to make things work out with him, even though my heart had already begun to harden towards him and hatred had begun to work its way through my veins and into my system.

I had finally gotten what I had wanted all along, only to find that I was no longer sure if I even wanted it after all. Steven had looked at me and said the words "I want you"- the very words I had always longed to hear from him. But now it was me who was no longer sure if I really wanted him.

Seven

Steven's disappearing act continued until several

weeks after our child was born. He did everything he could to hide from me, including shunning his friends and family members and even changing his phone number. Times were very hard for me. Nathan was there to support me during this time in my life, but I was still feeling very depressed and alone.

I reached out to Cain in an attempt to solicit his help. I was all alone with a newborn child and had no one I could really turn to. My mother had long wanted me to come and stay around where she lived, but she had, by this time, moved so far away and I just didn't have it in me to leave. My home was there, where I had grown up, and I didn't want to live the life of a single mother and all of the hardships that would entail.

It was a bright Saturday afternoon when I slowly pulled up into the driveway where Cain lived. I was so nervous I could barely breathe. I didn't see any cars parked in the driveway. It appeared that nobody was home. I slowly made my way down the little dirt road. I parked as far away from the house as I could, then slowly got out of the car.

I walked up to the house and knocked on the door. No answer. I waited for a moment. All was still and quiet. I went back to my truck and found a piece of paper and a pen that I found in the bottom of my purse. I wrote a quick note to Cain with my phone number attached to it. It was a message that he would go on to ignore completely.

After leaving my note for Cain, I then went back home. Afterward, Mia came over. I told her about the events of my day. Mia was not very happy with the situation. She had known Steven since they were kids and had even gone to school with him. She was a pushy type of girl.

After a bit, she looked at me and simply said "Come on."

We got in her car, and she drove over to Steven's house. He answered the door for her but then insisted that he didn't want to see either the child or me.

Mia then came back to the car and said: "Let's go."

"What's going on?" I asked.

"He not ready to see you or the child," she replied as she backed out of the driveway.

"What? Oh hell no! He is not going to do this to me and just turn us out like this. Turn around,"I said even as she continued driving down the road.

"No. Not now," she replied.

We continued back to my house. Life continued on like this for another couple of weeks until one day Mia finally got Steven on the phone. I heard her off in the distance arguing with him over the phone about how he needed to grow up as he had a child now and had responsibilities. After she had hung up the phone, she walked over in my direction.

"He wants to see you," she said.

"Oh, so now he wants to see us? I guess it's now convenient for him then?" Anger welled up within me even while excitement built up inside of me at the prospect of seeing Steven again.

It should have been him going out of his way for us. In reality, however, it was me that got into my pickup and strapped my six-week old child into her car seat and headed to Steven's house.

It was already dark when I pulled up into his driveway. I sat outside in the car for a minute, unsure of what to do. The porch light turned on, and I saw Steven appear in the doorway. I reached around to unbuckle my baby and cradled her in my arms.

I slowly got out of the car, walked up to the porch and then into the house. There were few lights on so it was a bit dark whenever I came in. Steven was sitting there on the couch. I walked and stood in front of him. He looked thoughtful. I just stood there holding the baby in my arms.

"Let me hold her," he said quietly as he extended out his arms.

I handed him the child, and he gazed into a miniature face nearly identical to his own. There was no way he could ever deny this child. He reached out to grab her hand, and Hope curled her hand around his finger.

"Such tiny hands and feet," he said as he continued to gaze thoughtfully into the child's face.

He looked at me for a moment then commented on my still slender figure and soft, smooth skin. One would think I would have been flattered by his words, but instead, I was offended. What was I supposed to look like, hideous just because I was now a mother?

He handed Hope back to me, and I sat beside him on the couch. We stayed together until very late that night and talked. I desired to stay there with him, as I couldn't bear to go home and be all alone, even if I did have my child with me to comfort me, but we hadn't yet established our relationship together after everything that had happened between us. Late that night around midnight, I made my way home with a deep sadness in my heart.

Steven stayed in constant contact with me after that night, and two weeks later we agreed that Steven would come and live with me in the home I was renting at the time.

My landlord stood outside on the porch with me as we talked. He was a tall man, still in good shape for his age- which I had guessed to be somewhere in his mid-fifties, or later- with white hair.

"Is he the father of the child?" he asked me.

I looked at him with an odd look. "Yes..." I replied.

Was that some kind of trick question? Who else would he be? Would I be moving in with some other guy? Still so naïve to the world around me, I hadn't ever considered any other possibility.

"That's fine. I know of the family he comes from," he said as he agreed to Steven staying there with me.

After he had given permission for Steven to move into the house with me, he talked to me for a couple of minutes longer. He then left.

I then went inside and began to cook some lunch- if you could really call what I was doing "cooking." I wouldn't develop any homemaking skills yet for some time to come.

Later that very same day Steven moved all of his things into the house, and we began to live there together. For the first time, I actually had real furniture in the home. I had moved out of Lenard's house with barely anything more than my clothes, a few dishes, silverware, and pots and pans that my mother had given me, as well as a twin-size bed that I had been sleeping on since I was about ten years old. After the baby had come I was gifted with the necessary equipment I would need- such as a high-chair, baby bathtub and crib from family members- so at least our child had not wanted for anything. As I had periodically bought baby clothes before she was even born, clothes were never a problem either.

I continued to strip, but it wasn't long before the profession began to wear on me. Steven continued working at his job the way he had before, yet I found myself bringing in more money than he was. He would watch the baby at night while I would go out and dance, coming home in the middle of the night reeking of cigarette smoke from working all night in the bar.

While it didn't necessarily bother me- at first, anyway- I was never able to feel a real deep love or attraction for Steven. I didn't need him. If anything, I sometimes loathed his presence in what I considered to be my home. Nonetheless, our relationship wasn't completely passionless. We were practically teenagers still, after all.

"Shhh! Hope is asleep!" I said one afternoon as Steven came up behind me and started kissing me on the neck, tickling me.

"Come on…" he attempted to coax me.

"Fine." I laughed as we made our way to the bed.

He pulled off his shirt and began to undress me. Hope was about four months old by now, and this would be the first time we had made love since she was born. Only a few moments later we were both naked under the sheets. He got on top of me and started talking in my ear as he began to move deep within me.

The sex this time around wasn't like it was before Hope was born. It had changed. I had changed. A couple of minutes in I just simply started to relax. I let my legs fall down casually as he kept thrusting into me at a steady pace.

Suddenly I felt something building within me. I didn't understand what was happening. There was just this good feeling that began to overwhelm my entire body. I started making a lot of noise as the tension kept building within me down below. I felt like I might explode and started crying out. Immediately afterward Steven stopped moving and looked up at me. Still breathing heavily, I just lay there, wondering what had just happened to me.

"Are you alright?" Steven asked. I just shook my head.

So this was it- an orgasm. I had never experienced anything like it before in my life. I wasn't sure how it had happened exactly, but I knew I liked it and wanted to experience the feeling again.

It took a while but eventually I learned that if I just lay down on my back and relaxed I could just simply enjoy him and focus on what he was doing to me. Most of the time I would eventually orgasm, feeling that wonderful sensation yet again.

Standing there in front of the full-length mirror in my sky-high heels and dancer's attire, I examined my ring in the mirror. I felt a tear escape from my eye. I didn't know how much longer I could keep this up. The birth of Hope had irrevocably changed my entire life. Everything was different. I saw the world through different eyes. I viewed sex differently from what the world had been preaching to me from the media, in the movies I saw, and the hip-hop music blaring from the speakers upstairs. They talked about sex like it was nothing. But how could it be so casual of a thing the way they claimed? Just look what it had done to my life.

I took off my ring and shoved it into my duffle bag before heading back upstairs to the bar. I couldn't wear it on stage without running off all of my potential customers, many of whom bought me drinks in the hopes of being the one that would take me home. It was a fantasy I sold them. That was what I got paid to do. But I didn't want to take that ring off. It was a part of who I was now. I was a mother and soon to be a wife.

The ring itself wasn't anything fancy. Bought from a pawn shop in town it had only cost about ten dollars. Getting Steven to propose was even more ridiculous. I envisioned he might get down on his knees or something, but instead, he just sat on the couch watching television while he tossed the ring in my direction. It was just *implied* that we were going to marry.

"I'll leave now so he can propose," Lenard said as he walked out the front door of our home, laughing.

I then turned on Steven. I crossed my arms in front of me and tapped my foot. "I'm waiting," I said.

He looked up at me with that smirk of his, yet remained seated on the couch. "Oh, whatever," I declared before starting to stomp off in the opposite direction.

"Ok, fine,"Steven said.

He then partially got down on one knee and put the ring on my finger. The play-acting only lasted for about thirty seconds, however, before he proceeded to plant himself right back on the couch to continue watching television. Secretly, I didn't really care for the dramatics of a traditional marriage proposal. I just couldn't resist giving him a hard time. We would go on to have a rather simple wedding anyway, but I wouldn't have had it any other way.

Bringing myself back to the present, I tried to concentrate on the lap-dance I was giving. The man I was dancing for grabbed my waist and attempted to get me to grind a little more intimately on him, but now that I had been awakened to the pleasures of the flesh I just couldn't do it.

I backed off a bit from him and, without a word, took his hands and placed them on each side of him. I gave him a naughty look to make him think I was really into it, that I was just play-acting and putting myself in charge of his pleasure, when secretly I just wanted to run away, to get away, to be anywhere but where I was at that moment. I just couldn't do it anymore.

I only lasted a couple more weeks working at night as an exotic dancer before I came home one evening and said I had quit.

"I can't go back ever again," I said as I talked with Steven that very next day.

I knew he didn't want me dancing anymore (an issue of male jealousy, I knew) but it was my dancing that kept paying the rent, as my income still surpassed his by a long way.

"We'll have to find someplace else to live and another way to survive. We can't afford to pay the rent here with my income alone," he said.

"I know."

So it was settled then. We'd live in the house while the rent was paid up. In the meantime, Steven began searching for another place to live. We'd stay in the spare bedroom in his grandparent's house in the meantime. We had a simple wedding by the lake a short time later, and Steven found us an old trailer house. He had it moved to the same place he had grown up as a child, to the same place where he lived when I first met him. When it was ready, we would move in and live together, as a family, with our child.

I'd like to say that it was all smooth sailing from there on out; that we lived together in wedded bliss and lived happily-ever-after. But to report such a thing would be but a fabrication of the truth.

In reality, our marriage would be rife with hatred, resentment, and regret that would nearly tear our lives apart more than once throughout the years that we would spend together.

Eight

$\mathcal{S}$teven worked hard to get us moved into our new

home, and Cain was there right beside him helping to
make having a place of our own a reality. It was a dump
and we would surely qualify as trailer trash, but at least
it would be a place of our own. There's only so much one
can take of living with their in-laws before any situation,
even a drastic one, begins to look like paradise.

Though Steven pressured me, I didn't go out
searching for a new job. I put in one application at a local
grocery store. The manager of the place had actually
called me, yet I declined, saying that I wasn't looking for
employment. We had a newborn. I believed that Steven
should be supporting us and no matter what his desires

were on the matter, I was determined to stay home and raise my child full- time.

"Did they call you about the job?" he asked me over the phone one afternoon while on his lunch break.

"Yes, they did."

"What did you tell them?"

"I said I wasn't interested."

"You need to call them back."

"No! I don't want a job. I want to take care of Hope," I told him. I then promptly hung up the phone before he could say another word. He didn't press the issue further.

Determined not ever to get pregnant again, I began taking hormonal birth control. Perhaps this combined with the hormonal cocktail already happening within my body after giving birth was what made me feel and act like a crazy person, or perhaps Steven's treatment of me over the years was finally catching up to me. No longer could I hold back all of the emotions of hatred and resentment I was feeling inside.

As soon as we had moved into our new home, we began to fight each other and yell at each other non-stop. A couple of nights I would stay up half the night crying, hating my life and hating the situation I found myself in. Steven couldn't deal with me and instead went to sleep on the couch. Now that I had a child with him I could no longer just up and walk away from him. Even if I walked away, we'd still have to deal with each other and have our lives entwined together- perhaps even more-so if we split apart than if we simply remained together and dealt with the hatred we felt, despite whatever ways we decided to express it.

"I hate you!" I yelled as I sent the chair soaring across the living room in his direction. He quickly dodged the chair, and it continued on its way until it smashed into the wall behind him. Now he was angry.

"Bitch!" He came charging in my direction and grabbed me by the hair, yanking my head back.

I reached up and slapped him across the face, chipping his tooth. He slapped me back, busting my lip. He let go of my hair, and I reached out for him, grabbing him by the shoulders. He grabbed me by the arm and threw me down on the couch. I was seething at this point and just simply screamed. He walked away, and I ran into the bedroom, slamming the door so hard behind me that the entire house shook. I leaned against the door and allowed myself to simply slide downwards as I began to cry. I don't know how long I stayed there as time had no meaning to me anymore. Things couldn't go on any longer this way.

I regretted the decisions I had made. I regretted everything.

The next evening Steven and I sat on the front stairs talking. We still felt love for each other, it was true, but I was emotionally overwrought, and we were fighting so much I just didn't know what to do.

It was a calm conversation that we had that night. I told him I would leave for a while. I said I didn't know for certain when I would come back.

"You're leaving Hope here," he told me.

I just looked at him quietly for a moment. "Ok." We then sat together for a while before going back inside.

I had just turned twenty years old at this point. I had no knowledge of life beyond the small box I had lived in- a box that my father was primarily responsible for keeping me in. If only he had taught me something about the world, about life, maybe things for me would have turned out differently. As it was, I hated him for what he had done to me growing up, for the way that he had kept me in ignorance without teaching to me the things I needed to know before going out into the world.

I called up my mother the next day, and she sent me a one-way plane ticket to come and see her. The morning after that Steven drove me to the airport.

"Maybe it's a sign you shouldn't be leaving," he said as he attempted to start up his truck, only to find that it wouldn't start for him.

He then borrowed a car from one of his relatives. It appeared that it would have problems starting up as well, but eventually he got it going. He drove me up the airport. I'll never forget that feeling when I looked back as I was checking my things before boarding. I looked back to see Steven standing there, sadness and love for me in his eyes. I felt inside that I shouldn't be leaving, that I shouldn't be going anywhere. I almost broke down in tears, and the only thing I really wanted to do was to run back into his arms. But I didn't.

I boarded the plane that day and didn't look back. I was going alone. I had left Hope with him, as we had previously agreed. I needed to heal. I couldn't even be the mother I was supposed to be to her if things did not change. This was the only way.

It was only on about day two out of my two-week absence that Steven began to turn on me. I had been talking to him on the phone every night when all of a sudden he started to become a belligerent asshole to me, telling me how much better Hope was doing in the care of his family members. By day five he had cut off my cell phone and refused to speak to me whenever I would borrow my mother's or grandmother's phone and attempt to call him.

Things had turned ugly. I had to go home. I had no money of my own and neither did I have transportation. I waited there at my mother's until she and my grandparents drove me all the way back home- a two-day drive.

Whenever I got home two days later, the house was a wreck. Steven was at work when I arrived. He wouldn't tell me where Hope was. I was treated as an outcast and shunned by his relatives. Even Cain himself was hostile to me.

"Are you staying in the house?" Cain asked me when I came down to his house to talk to him, looking for Steven and Hope. Technically we were still living on his land, as it would not be our land for at least another two years to come. I shook my head yes. Where else could I go?

"Can I use your phone?"I asked him.

"You can't call Steven on that phone."

"I need to talk to him."

Without saying anything, Cain dialed Steven on his phone and briefly talked to him. He then looked up at me, standing there in his kitchen. "He says he doesn't want to talk to you."

I didn't say anything more. Before I left Cain at least asked if I had enough to eat. I just shook my head yes and walked out the door to find some other phone to use. What the willing giver he was.

I stayed in our home alone that evening as Steven never came back. Around eight 8:00 that same evening I heard someone pulling up outside our home. I looked out the window as a man I had never seen before came up to the door and knocked. I opened the door as he served me with a bunch of papers.

"What's this?" I asked him.

"Divorce papers I believe, ma'am," he replied. He then turned to get back into his car.

When he had gone, I went back inside and sat down and looked at everything. It was the craziest bunch of nonsense I had ever seen in my entire life. He accused me of every wrong-doing under the sun, save for adultery, and made me out to look like some crazy madwoman that threatened his very life. The papers said he wanted to dissolve our marriage and take Hope away from me. I threw the papers on the floor and walked away, unfeeling, into the next room to lie down.

I didn't sleep that night. Not once did I hardly close my eyes. I finally got up out of bed at 7:30 the next morning and called my mother and grandparents, who were still in town, and told them what was going on.

The next evening I went over to Lenard's and showed him the papers. "It's just lawyer talk- standard procedure," he said to me when he was done reading through everything. Not that he would help me any. The only person Lenard ever cared about was himself.

My mother would help me, but, as was always typical with her, she wanted me to stay with her instead of going back to our home. I refused. I said I wanted to come home.

"You want to go right back to a place where you are unwanted?" she said to me with disbelief as we were riding off together towards where she and my grandparents were staying. "Wake up! He doesn't want you! Nobody there wants you!"

"Please just either take me back home or let me out of the car!" I told them. "If you don't want to take me back then I'll just walk but let me out!"

My grandfather then stopped and turned the car around to take me back home- to the very place that I was so unwanted.

As it so happened, Steven came back to me that very evening. I was sitting there on the bed in my wedding dress enjoying the feeling of being feminine when I heard the unmistakable sound of his truck pulling up outside. I quickly discarded the wedding dress and threw it on the foot of the bed, embarrassed to be caught in it.

He came in and talked to me for approximately five minutes before proceeding to tell me how horny he was. He thought I had gotten undressed just for him. Allowing him to think it true, I allowed him to make love to me that night.

The next day I told him the first thing he was going to do was drop his case against me for divorce. He found it wasn't so easy to do as his lawyer was unwilling just to drop the case, claiming concern for our child as her reason. I was certain concern for her pocketbook was the real reason, but I just waited in the car while Steven, accompanied by Lenard, negotiated with her.

Eventually, Lenard got her to drop the case entirely so Steven and I could reconcile and quietly go on with our lives. Years later Steven would tell me that he didn't know what was even written up in those papers. His relatives were pressing him to divorce me, and the lawyer just went to typing away a whole bunch of things. I didn't believe him, really, but his story became more credible later on when Lenard backed up what he was saying. Lenard may have been a lot of things, but he wasn't the type to fabricate that sort of story.

Did it matter if Steven knew what was in those papers? In my mind, yes, it did. It made all the difference in how I viewed him and in just how far I was willing to trust him. But it didn't matter. My mind was made up. All the recent events had just reinforced in my mind just how much of a mistake I had made by becoming a mother and by getting married. I was determined that I would never make that mistake again.

A couple of months later, right on my twenty-first birthday, I sat across from my gynecologist in a consultation to undergo surgery for sterilization. My doctor was a man of Asian descent and of average height. I found myself to be comfortable with him. He wasn't my first choice for a doctor, but he was the one with the earliest available opening. Looking back, I'm glad that he ended up being my doctor. Given my age, another doctor might have hassled me more or flat-out refused to do what I wanted to have done. Even to this day, I am thankful that he ended up being the one I saw.

He was very agreeable and understanding. I informed him that I was aware of all of my birth control options, but I was, without a doubt, never going to have any more children and I wanted something permanent and reliable that I didn't have to ever worry about again.

I informed him of the procedure that I wanted to have done. He then consented to do the procedure on me and began to map out on the calendar when everything would take place. Afterward, he turned around one last time towards me.

"Are you sure? You're so young!" He said.

"I've never been more sure of anything in my life."

A month later I was being wheeled back into the operating room where I would say goodbye to my fertility forever.

Nine

Luckily we were already living in a time where

women had more options for sterilization than the traditional method of cutting into you and tying your tubes. I chose a non-invasive procedure available to me and was back on my feet within a couple of days, with only minimal cramping and discomfort during the healing phase.

I'm not so sure Steven wanted me to undergo the operation. Before they took me back for surgery, he looked at me and said, "Are you sure about this?" There was an underlying sadness in his voice.

"Yes," I told him.

I had never been surer about anything in my entire life. Nor did it matter to me what he wanted me to do. If society and the law allowed him to treat me the way he had treated me then why should it matter? Why should he get a say in such an intimate and important matter such as this when I, the child-bearer, received no protections for being the one who bore the consequences of the sex act? He didn't bear the consequences, how could it be his decision?

After the procedure, I began questioning my life. A few months earlier I had started attending online college courses. I was convinced it was the only path I should be on. I had to empower myself to keep myself from ever getting hurt again- either by Steven or any other man. I majored in legal studies, then in psychology and I learned the meaning of the word "patriarchy." I was on the path to becoming a right bitch.

Partly spurred on by Lenard's false teachings of history and partly by my own experiences with Steven and some of the men I had to deal with during my days as an exotic dancer, I began to believe that women's empowerment was the only way to go. I believed that all men must be the same way- oppressors of women. I was particularly convinced that the men of the past must have been just as terrible to women as Lenard had been to my mother and me.

There were things that I knew about Lenard and my mother's relationship. I knew that he was a good twelve or thirteen years apart in age from my mother. She was just a teenager when she met and fell in love with him. At first, he gave her the world, only to turn into a completely different person after she married him and had a child with him. Wasn't that quite typical of men? They would lure you in by helping you out, gifting you with roses and charming you only to turn around and disappear on you one day or all of a sudden morph into a completely different person.

Steven and I continued in our relationship, but I kept him at arm's length. I was still very distrustful of him and was always convinced that he might turn on me at any moment. *Screw him. I must do for myself,* I thought.

But something just didn't feel right inside. This isn't what I had always wanted. This isn't what my instincts told me. I wanted to be feminine; I wanted to be a woman. I wanted a man to love me, be stronger than me in this life and take care of me.

But what other way was there? Men had never taken care of women. Men were always oppressing women and then when the children inevitably came along they too became one more weapon men could use to control and manipulate us with. But at least *those* days, the days of worrying about pregnancy and babies that is, were behind me.

I felt inside of me that I had something to share with the world. I wanted to change things! I felt this compelling drive inside of me to do so. But what would I change? I mean, I knew what I felt was wrong inside but as of yet what solution was there?

"I want to do something!" I exclaimed to Steven one day while I paced around the living room.

"And you can," he said. "I'll support you in whatever you want to do."

"I don't know what to do yet. That's why I started college in the first place, because I don't know anything and in order to change things I have to be educated. I'd just be some discontent fool otherwise."

Steven loved me; that much was obvious. I loved him too, but I still felt trapped in my current situation. I didn't trust him- or any man for that matter. I always felt like he might turn on me at any moment. I felt like I was living in enemy territory, surrounded by all of his relatives, and always felt the need to watch my back lest they shoot me down or injure me somehow.

I continued to dig into my studies while caring for Hope at home. I did feel guilty somewhere deep down in my heart. I felt that I was robbing Hope of the attention that I should have been paying her; like I was robbing both her and myself of something very valuable and precious. After all, she was growing bigger every day and all the time I spent focusing on my studies and not on her was time I knew I was never going to get back.

"But at least you're there with her. That's what's important," my mother said to me one day over the phone.

"I guess. But it still just doesn't feel right though. I don't pay her enough attention. I don't feel like I'm a very good mother."

"Just focus on finishing school that way you can get your degree and make sure you're using birth control, so you don't have to worry about any more babies for the time being. And what's Steven going to do when you have all those degrees anyways? Is he still going to be stuck working at that dead-end job of his while you're out there establishing yourself in a well-paying career?"

I didn't know what Steven would do, nor did I really care. I was for women's empowerment all the way, even if I ended up making more money than him. The one thing that she and all of my other relatives didn't know, however, was that I no longer *had* any need for birth control.

So it was one night while doing some psychology homework that I read something that I had never even heard before. I read that men used to have to financially support their wives and that mothers did have rights to their children upon divorce, even more so than they do in our modern times, on the basis that they were their children's primary caretakers- the same as I was with Hope.

This started something inside of me. I started to question everything that I had been told in our modern times about feminism and women's empowerment. Perhaps there was a reason why I felt all the things I felt inside- feelings about how something feminine inside of me was being repressed.

I started researching some things and concepts over the internet, and more and more information and facts that I had never heard about or known before were presented to me. I learned the term "anti-feminist." It was an odd term to me at first. I didn't know there even *were* people against feminism, except for maybe those extreme religious types you see on television- the real nut-cases- that did things such as forcing thirteen-year-old girls to bear children and other extreme things such as "honor killings." That was all I had ever heard about before.

I started reading some anti-feminist books. Yes, there were actually anti-feminist books out there! It was interesting, all these things I was reading about and learning. It confirmed that my feminine instincts were not wrong; I had just been taught to suppress them by the society around me. I didn't know there was any other way to be other than what the culture around me had been telling me.

I knew I couldn't continue on this path of women's empowerment. It made women hate and distrust men, and it made men do and feel the same in return towards women. I cried when I thought about finishing out college and starting on the path towards some career. It didn't feel right. I wanted to be a woman; I needed to be a woman.

Seeing as though I could not continue on, I dropped out of college. It's not that I felt education or college was wrong. Perhaps in some ways, it would have been better if I had simply finished. But it wasn't where I was at during that particular point in my life. My family, my child, and my homemaking were the most important to me.

Driving back home one day, Steven and I were all alone in the truck. I leaned over and laid my head on his chest. I then looked up at him.

"I trust you," I said softly to him.

"You don't know what it means to me to hear you say that," he replied.

That moment seemed to change our relationship. I was no longer on some crusade for empowerment. I no longer held any contempt for the male sex or fathers in general. I still knew that things were not right in our modern society and I knew that male-female relationships were not good in our world today. But I felt that they could be better, and maybe I could be part of some cause, yet unknown to me, to make them better.

Perhaps this unknown cause, the cause to make things right between the sexes and to lift up masculinity and femininity and the differences between us- differences that were good and natural- was what I had been searching for all along. Perhaps this was my calling.

I continued to dive into reading and reviewing both feminist and anti-feminist literature. I also loved to take the time to review the books I read on various social media sites. I began to wonder just how I would go about making a difference.

I did some small-scale political talk on social media, but I still really wanted to start something of my own. Not long after, I met Edna. The two of us got along real well and started our own websites and campaigned online together. We continued to be partners up until the time she turned against us a couple of years later and disassociated herself with the campaign entirely. By that time a large following had already gathered around us and so I just continued on without her.

We had started a good thing together. Fed up with the talk of women's rights around us that simply centered on the workforce, I had proposed the idea one day that we campaign instead for the rights of us women that wished to remain in the home. I proposed that we stand up for the rights of the traditional woman- and thus the term *Traditional Woman's Rights Activist* was born.

Ten

$\mathcal{L}$ife resumed on at a fairly normal pace for me after I

started my political cause. I kept myself busy around the house and attempted to learn all I could about traditional homemaking skills. I learned to cook and clean better than I ever had before and I delighted in simply being the "traditional woman" with the old-fashioned viewpoints that I was constantly writing about on my blog. I cared for Hope and as she got older I delighted in taking her to and from school, watching how she would change and learn to interact better with the world around her as she grew up and got older.

Cain moved away out of town for a couple of years, and I felt a sense of relief. Finally, it was like I had finally gotten rid of some enemy. Due to our strained relationship and the things he had done to me in the past, I felt very little love for him. In fact, I almost felt this hatred inside for him and loathed his very existence and presence in our lives. He didn't come around much nor did I want him to. No other person had ever put so much antagonism between Steven and I the way he had. Only once had he ever came to see Hope after she was born, after Steven and I got together. Things were either going to be done his way, or he would apparently have nothing to do with us at all.

So it was with a great sense of annoyance that I accepted the fact that Cain would be moving back home again. Reportedly the new job wasn't all he thought it would be for him, and perhaps, though I cannot say for sure, there were other personal issues at play as well. Soon Cain was back home, working to rebuild his business that he had created for himself over the years.

The months passed, and I did my best to ignore his very existence. I had minimal contact with him, except whenever he happened to be around, which wasn't very often- thankfully. I was doing very well at ignoring him, until one cold December morning a few months later when the temperature began to drop into the single digit range. Living far enough South, the temperature rarely got so cold.

We had no water; we had nothing. Everything was frozen solid. Cain came up and spent the day unfreezing our pipes. He had spent many hours in the past helping Steven to work on our home so we could live in it. But this time was different. Somehow it just seemed a little more personal. I was there alone with him. Steven was at work, and Hope was at school. Cain went above and beyond what was necessary, even unfreezing pipes to unnecessary items such as the ice-maker. It took him a long time, working out in the below-freezing weather, to get everything working right for me.

As the pipes were being unfrozen, I began to work on the pile of dishes sitting in the sink that was beginning to spill over onto the countertop. All of a sudden one of the pipes under the sink sprung a major leak. Water began to rush everywhere. I leaned my head out the door beside where Cain was working only a few feet away.

"Um, the sink…It's leaking…" I said shyly.

He looked up at me without saying anything. I smiled slightly then turned around to walk back inside.

He came inside and into the kitchen. He crouched down to examine the pipes below the sink and began to work on them. I observed him as he worked. I wasn't sure exactly his age, he was somewhere in his mid-forties, but suddenly I began to notice how very attractive he was. He was still so dark, not even showing a hint of gray anywhere, and nothing about his figure had been lost to him over time. He wasn't particularly tall, but he was well-built.

My eyes traveled downward towards where he was working. His hands were so rough and work-worn. *The hands of a man*, I thought. Something began to stir inside of my heart that day. Slowly my thoughts and feelings towards him began to change. There was something innocently romantic about that moment in time, something that would stay with me in my mind for many years to come.

I watched him for a moment at a distance. I admired him yet while I feared him. He had caused so much pain to my life before; he had caused so much hurt. He had scared me before.

My mind traveled back to the night right after me and Steven's marriage, right after we had first moved into our new home. We didn't have that home anymore, of course. We had a much nicer home at this point even though we still lived on the same plot of land, right next to Cain. I had sent him a particularly nasty message earlier that day. That evening he came bursting through the door yelling at me, causing me to flee to the safety of the bathroom before he finally retreated- after he had given me an earful.

Was he still capable of that same behavior now? I didn't know, but I felt that I was safe enough with him there now.

"Everything should be working now." I started and looked up at him, his voice having awoken me from my reverie. "You might want to put a fan under there to let everything dry faster."

I gave him a shy smile as I nodded my head. "OK."

He went back outside to finish what he was doing, coming back in every once in a while when he needed to access or work on something inside. I went back to doing the dishes.

Cain had long ago made the offer that I could bring Hope down to play in his yard if I wished. It's true that his yard was much nicer than ours. Though the back of his house was wooded, his front yard was nice and flat, and the grass grew well. I had never taken him up on his offer, however, given the way I had felt about him over all the years past.

But it seemed like something had changed now. Often, usually in the afternoons when Cain was around his house working, I would go down with Hope to play and maybe make a bit of small talk with Cain. Whenever there was severe weather, we took shelter in his home. He had never done anything bad or inappropriate towards me. I began to like him and looked forward to any time when I could be around him. I began to secretly admire him from afar.

It was true that there were times when he seemed a bit distant, but I just chalked that up to typical masculine behavior and didn't think much about it. He was good and friendly to me and took care of me whenever I needed something. He developed more of a relationship with Steven after coming back home, and he was often up at our house, whether he was just simply dropping by or on a mission of some sort, or working. He and Steven would sometimes even work together.

One day he walked through the door showing me some of the guitars he had been collecting. He showed one of them to me, a beautiful Spanish guitar. I looked at it for a minute, admiring it, when all of a sudden he handed it to me and said, "You can have it."

I squealed. I was delighted. I had never been gifted with anything like that before. I sat down and started messing with it, and both Cain and Steven walked back outside to look at something, what I don't know. I was preoccupied with my new gift.

I would go on to cherish that gift for years to come, especially in the sad and lonely moments ahead when I would miss Cain's presence in my life.

Though I began to be comfortable with Cain and even came to like him- perhaps, even though I hadn't acknowledged it yet, even to love him- there were still so many things left unspoken between us. Maybe he never thought about it, but I did. There was still this subtle feeling of resentment deep inside of me due to the happenings of the past. I wanted to get over it so badly, but it was difficult as there were still so many unanswered questions. But how could I talk to him about it? Where would I begin?

Sometimes, when I would feel that same old resentment creep up into my consciousness, I would avoid coming around for a while- but I wouldn't stay gone for long. I would miss Cain too much. I would soon come back around, tamping down the negative feelings I felt inside.

Eleven

Over the years it sometimes seemed to me that Cain

was able to read my soul; as if he had looked into my heart and understood me- perhaps even better than I understood myself. Perhaps he even paid more attention to me than what Steven did.

It's true that he wasn't always around, but I guess as soon as I started to be OK with his presence, and Steven allowed him to come around more, he did. I had been writing my blog for a couple of years at this point. I continued to play around a bit on social media. I had already added Cain long ago as a "friend" on my Facebook account.

Of course, Cain was always more of the private type. Rarely did he ever say anything on social media.

He wasn't the type to go posting his entire life or day online for everyone to read about. But since he was always working, it was doubtful he had the time for such foolishness anyway. So it was a bit of a surprise whenever I started seeing signs that he might indeed be reading my blog.

I was careless in those days. I didn't think I'd ever get much popularity, so I posted some things to my personal page. Boy was I wrong! It didn't take long before my public pages gained a lot of popularity. I was running an anti-feminist campaign, and all of a sudden feminist rivals began making pages against me and criticizing me. Eventually, they ran me off of social media, and I closed down everything to focus solely on my blog writings. In the end, it worked out better that way anyway, as dealing with social media just became tiring. I retreated into myself more and focused solely on housework and writing articles whenever something came to my mind.

And something always did come to my mind. I'd see or hear something, and it would begin to form thoughts in my head. Sometimes those thoughts were good and sometimes they were bad. Either way, my writings gave me an outlet to express all of the emotions and feelings that I held inside. I gained a large following in a short amount of time.

One particular day I was writing about my thoughts on sex and childbirth. I wrote about how ridiculous it was that men these days went around saying stupid expressions like "we're pregnant," even though biology dictated that only *women* actually carried life inside of them. I described how I felt so precious and vulnerable having a baby and how I loved the feeling of being invaded when my husband and I would have sex.

Cain was at the house later that evening. The weather was cold outside, and he was wearing that tan jacket of his. I always thought he looked so good in that jacket. It made him look a bit rougher, a bit more masculine. Before leaving, he turned around and gave me this smirk. Did he know something? Was he reading what I was writing?

Cain was always the sneaky type; nobody could ever know what the man was really up to. I thought I understood him, though. Over time I learned all the various little quirks about him- including how to tell when he was lying. He seemed to pay so much attention to me as well- without ever making it obvious, of course. He would never admit that he paid any attention to me. Perhaps it was better that way. Perhaps it made him more attractive in my eyes. And perhaps it was because I believed Cain truly cared about me that what would go on to happen next came as such a shock to me.

There's never truly been a time in our marriage that Steven and I did not fight. Yes, I loved him. I loved him very much. We had a great life together, including a great sex life as well. I certainly kept him happy in that regard. But there was still this part of me that hated my life, and even after all years gone by, I would sometimes feel trapped. Sometimes I wrote about my feelings on my blog.

I would write about how, yes, I *was* happy, but at the same time I was also so dreadfully unhappy. I supposed that all females felt that same discontent on the inside. Perhaps it was just in the nature of women to feel that way. I wrote how I would indeed leave if I could, but it was my financial dependency upon my husband that kept me here in the marriage. It kept our relationship stable throughout all of the ups and downs, the good and the bad- just like the vows spoken in a marriage ceremony. Perhaps our ancestors knew that, I reasoned, and that's why patriarchal societies always became the most powerful and produced the most stable of family arrangements.

"I know that I would probably leave if I could," I wrote on my blog. I went on to say, "that is one of the reasons why I have declined to take on paid employment since I married. It keeps our relationship more stable."

In this way, I promoted my presence in the home, even if a part of me inside wished for my own independence to enable me to leave or at least do my own thing whenever I became unhappy.

But there were still questions I needed answers to, so one day I asked Steven to ask Cain to come and talk to me. I was also ready to leave Steven. I couldn't take being there anymore.

"It's never going to happen," Steven said calmly one afternoon as he walked in through the front door.

"What do you mean? Did you ask him?"

"Yes." Steven was sitting down on the couch at this point, looking thoughtful. "He won't come. He seemed a bit uncomfortable whenever I asked him about it."

I didn't say anything, but simply sank to the floor, my back against the wall. *What? How had this happened? Why? What had I done?*

Anger welled up within me. I hated everything. I didn't know what I was going to do or where I was going to go, but I had to get away.

I packed up a small bag of things and started walking down the road. It was wintertime, and there was snow on the ground- a rare occurrence in this part of the country. But I didn't care. I kept walking.

Steven got in the jeep and pulled up beside me. I didn't want to get in the jeep with him, but I did. I was going to have him take me to Lenard's, but then the thought of it made me sick. Leaving made me sick. I would be all alone and trapped in a dump, leaving behind all of the comforts of home.

Steven drove us down to the store, and we talked along the way. I didn't have much to say, but mainly just sat staring out the window with a mixture of both resentment and sadness welling up within me. I ended up coming back home with him that afternoon.

That evening I pulled out a fresh bottle of blush wine from the cabinet. It had been so long since I had even touched alcohol that I couldn't even remember what being buzzed felt like, so when my body began to vibrate all over after a couple of drinks it made me paranoid at first, but then I relaxed into the feeling.

Somehow that evening, after a few drinks, I ended up in bed with Steven. I passionately clung to him. I rolled around with him, releasing all of the anger, fear, sadness, and love that I felt. It was as if every emotion just rolled into one and I kept grabbing on to him.

Suddenly the most intense feeling of pleasure I had yet ever to know started coming over me. I exploded with emotion; I exploded from the physical sensations overcoming me. So intense was it that it caused me to scream out as I let everything I was feeling inside be released.

Afterward, it was like I had changed. I looked over at Steven and felt love for him once again. We'd had a very passionate sex life together over the years. I did always love him and had faithfully followed him, but I had never felt anything like that before. It seemed to rekindle our relationship- at least for the time being.

About a week later Cain was up at the house. He took Hope down to his house to let her play, as I had told him it was Ok. Hope jumped into the passenger seat of his truck, elated to be going to down to grandpa's house to play. She always loved being around her grandfather.

I decided to walk down myself a few minutes later. Joey left as soon as I walked up to the house. Cain was sitting on his front porch. He seemed distant and moody. Hope was playing with a sticky-hand toy on the front porch, dirtying it all up and having the time of her life.

I wanted to say something to Cain, but I couldn't think of where to begin. Either way, I felt uncomfortable and unwelcome. Perhaps I was just imagining it? I didn't know, but I began to feel that there was no place for me there in his life, so after a couple of minutes I just walked away and went back to the house.

But I knew it wasn't all just my imagination. Even Steven himself reported to me that Cain was acting differently. He didn't want to help Steven with anything the way he had in the past and wasn't really talking to him all that much anymore.

Steven did manage to solicit his help one evening to install our new front door, however. It was actually a door that Cain had given us. It was much nicer than our old front door, as it had a pretty decorative window- unlike our last one which was just plain white with no window.

Cain didn't act as though he wanted to be there. He helped with the door, but he just had this demeanor about him that was a bit hard to describe.

While the two men were working on the door, a severe storm began to form outside. It was just starting to rain, and the lightning was becoming more frequent whenever Cain left to go back home. Steven finished up with the doorknob by himself, while I entreated him to please hurry as the storm was beginning to scare me. He finished with the doorknob just as a tornado warning was issued.

We went down to Cain's house the same as we had many times over the years whenever bad weather would hit. Steven and Hope walked in the door, and I came in a few paces behind them.

I stopped right at the threshold whenever I saw the look in Cain's eyes as he looked up at me. I had never seen such a cold stare of hate like that from him before. I had never seen such a look of utter contempt in his eyes.

Joey abruptly stalked past me out the door. He then got in his car and left. We came and sat down on the couch until the storm passed. Cain made some small talk, but it seemed a bit forced. Later even Steven himself said, "I felt as though we were intruding somehow," whenever he spoke of that night. I felt like I might break down in tears.

So hurt was I that I didn't come back for months. Spring came and the trees sprang to life with fresh leaves, putting up a natural barrier between our house and Cain's. But I could still see and smell the smoke rising from his backyard whenever he'd light up a fire to burn his trash. I could still hear him as he worked around the yard and his house.

I wished I could be around and quietly sit as I used to while he worked. Something happened inside of me as I began to miss him and think more of him. Sometimes at night I would begin to cry. I would pick up the Spanish guitar he had given me and strum on it a bit. It reminded me of him. It was special to me. I would then carefully place it back in the corner of the bedroom and just sit quietly for a while. I felt as though something was missing inside of my heart.

As Springtime began to transform into Summer, words, so poetic in my mind, began to come to me. I sat down to write my thoughts of Cain and published them in a public blog article. I called him a "man" and I praised him for all of his accomplishments.

> *If I could sum up*
> *what I think of you, I would*
> *say that in all ways you are a*
> *man. You've done the work of*
> *a real man. You built your*
> *home with your own hands.*
> *Both directly and indirectly*
> *you've given so much to me...*
> *If by some chance of*
> *fate you ever read this I don't*
> *want you to ever think that*
> *what I feel is of a romantic*
> *nature- it's not. It is my*
> *husband that I love...*

My poetic musings continued on as I then wrote for him:

*...At times I have
seen in your face an
expression and in your eyes a
light that leaves no doubt that
your thoughts are every bit
those of a man's. I have
oftentimes found your intense
perusal and scrutiny of both
myself and the situation to be
more than a bit unnerving. At
times I feel you can read my
thoughts...*

*...It's that soft look in
your eyes when you talk to me
and those knowing smiles that
you give me. With one look
you can make me want to run
and hide...*

Indeed, the man made me nervous. At times he
even scared me, but I found that it intrigued me. I
blushed as I wrote the words for him, all the while

insisting to myself and the world at large that it wasn't romantic. But something inside of me knew that it was.

Three days later Cain caught my dog, a four-pound Chihuahua that we had bought about two months earlier. It was running around in his yard. He scooped it up and put it in the truck with him and pulled up to our house.

I was alone with Hope at the time, being that it was a Friday afternoon and Steven was still at work. My heart soared whenever I looked out the door and saw Cain get out of his truck. He carried our little dog in his left arm.

Hope raced out the door yelling "grandpa!" whenever she saw him.

My heart began to pound in my chest as he walked up onto the front porch. As he got closer, I opened up the door. He had a twinkle in his eyes as he reached out to hand me the little dog. I took the dog from his arms.

"Didn't want him to get run over," he said. He looked very pleased. He had never done anything like this before.

Too nervous to even speak, I smiled shyly and slowly began to shut the door. Hope was still on the front porch.

"Got to go to the store," Cain said to her as he walked back down the stairs.

I continued to peer through the window from behind the closed door as he got into his truck and drove away. How my heart longed for him to take me with him.

Twelve

$\mathcal{T}$he next day, a beautiful and sunny Saturday

afternoon, Cain came up to help Steven work on his
truck. I remember watching the two of them outside.
Cain seemed to be in a very good mood as the two men
worked together underneath the truck. I was elated.

I got up the nerve to come outside a few minutes
before Cain left. I didn't say anything. I was very shy
and could barely even look at him. Steven was still
working and needed me to hold a rope for him. He then
asked Cain, who was about to step into his truck to
leave, to come and help him unknot it.

Cain came up right beside me and grabbed the
rope, so close to where my own hand was already
holding it. I kept my eyes downcast and focused on the

rope. His hands were only a few inches from my own as he worked. I examined his hands the same as I had on that cold winter's day so long ago. They were still so strong looking; still so masculine and work-worn. The work overalls Cain had on only added to the effect he was having on me.

I shyly raised my head to look up at Cain. He kept his eyes on the rope and the work he was doing. He had an amused smile on his face as if he knew I was looking at him but was trying not to notice. I was so mesmerized by him. I'm quite sure I blushed profusely.

After we were done with the rope, I walked around to the side of the house, looking for something. Not finding what I was looking for, I instead just stood in the front yard as Cain got in his truck to leave. I kept my eyes downcast, looking off to the side as he drove away. I was still so shy around him, and he still made me so nervous.

I had finally persuaded Steven, after many years, to get me a screen door the way I had been begging him to do since practically the beginning of our marriage. The next weekend we headed into town. We looked at a few doors. I was content to get just a simple wooden one, but if he was going to buy one, he related to me, he was going to get the best one possible. That was fine with me. He picked out a nice-looking one that would match well with the outside of our house. We then headed back home.

The weekend after that Steven called up Cain to ask him to come help put the door up. Cain had been working in his yard. He came up immediately.

Earlier that day I had been upset. Cain hadn't been around for a while, and there was talk about him moving away. The prospect of Cain moving away saddened me greatly. While there was an undertone of romance to the entire situation, I was still at the stage of seeing Cain as a father figure. Earlier in the day, I had been crying to Steven.

"...But he's going to move away; then he'll be gone," I said as the tears coursed down my face. "I might not ever see him again."

Steven didn't say much of anything. He got out the booklet of directions for assembling the screen door then called Cain, asking for his help.

Steven lightly patted me on the shoulder whenever Cain walked through the door. It was a gesture meant to tell me that he knew how much Cain's presence there meant to me and that he had brought him up there for me.

While the two men were standing around the table looking at the directions together, I came out of the laundry room with a basket of clean laundry. Cain looked down at me as I gave him a shy smile. His expression was so serious. I wondered if I had done something wrong. Was he upset with me?

The two men worked together on the door while I sat on the couch folding laundry. "We might know what we're doing; we might not,"Cain said, laughing slightly. I smiled at him, and he walked back outside to continue working. I picked up the little dog and walked outside, petting him as I watched Cain outside working.

"What have you been up to, April?"he said, attempting to strike up some light conversation with me as he worked.

"Um, nothing," I replied shyly.

That was the reply I usually gave him, given how shy I was and how nervous he would make me every time I was around him. Without fail, I would always blush every time he asked me that question. "Nothing" was the only reply I ever found to give him- not because I wasn't ever busy with anything, but because I found small talk to be tedious and difficult.

I walked back inside with the dog. The door was nearly completely assembled at this point. Both Steven and Cain were standing outside on the front porch. Steven stood off to the left, with Cain right in front of the door facing towards me.

"See any daylight under there, April?" Cain said casually, though there seemed to be a touch of underlying humor and cockiness to his voice.

Avoiding his gaze, I looked down to the bottom of the screen door. It looked to be completely sealed off. I shook my head "no." When I looked back up at him, I jumped slightly. He was giving me a cold blank stare. There was literally nothing in his eyes. It shocked me, and I put my hands over my mouth and smiled shyly, suppressing a giggle. He was messing with me!

144

The screen door finally having been assembled, Cain was getting ready to leave. It was in the middle of summer at this point, so we had the door open still. Steven stood inside just off to my left, and Cain stood just outside the door a few feet away, almost directly in front of me. He and Steven were talking casually. I just stood there listening and smiling demurely.

At some point during the conversation, Cain fixed his gaze and attention on me. So intense was his focus that I began to feel uncomfortable. His feet and entire body were pointed in my direction. He then put his right foot out in front of him, as if frozen in his steps, like he was about to advance on me. He intimidated me.

I kept smiling at him, waiting for him to say something. Was he not going to say anything? What was he doing? His eyes were blank and expressionless; his face was stoic and hard. I looked over at Steven, who was still talking to Cain, with an expression that said "Hello!?" but he just kept right on talking. Cain would look over at Steven here and there to nod his head or say "yeah" in response to something that Steven was saying. He would then fix his attention and gaze hard back on me.

Eventually, I couldn't take the heat anymore and ran off into the bedroom. I heard Steven and Cain outside talking for a minute until Cain said to him "…Alright, see you later." and headed home.

I laid there curled up on the bed for a while. He had stirred something inside of me, both intriguing and frightening me.

Later that night I was talking to Steven about Cain. "I'm scared," I told him. "I'm afraid that he will try to manipulate me or something; possibly even seduce me. Perhaps he might even try to seduce me as a way of trying to get rid of me."

Steven just laughed at me.

About a week later I decided I would message Cain. I had never attempted to reach out to him personally in such a way before, but I wanted to try. I was shy and nervous at the prospect. It was about 8:00 at night when I finally got up the nerve to send my text message to him. I imagined him being at home alone relaxing when it came to him. It seemed somehow innocently romantic- perhaps even a bit mischievous. I wrote to him:

> *I'm confused.*
> *Have I done something*
> *wrong? Do you disapprove of*
> *me or something? I don't*
> *mean anything dishonorable*
> *by this message but you have*
> *always just been so special to*
> *me and I miss you. Though*
> *you have been mean and cruel*
> *to me sometimes I miss you*
> *terribly and it hurts me.*

My heart raced a hundred miles an hour when I hit the "send" button on my phone. He ended up ignoring my message. Later that next evening I told Steven I sent Cain a message. He went and burst through Cain's front door asking to see the message. Cain showed him.

Steven came home a few minutes later, thinking it to be cute. He said he asked Cain what he was doing to me that day. His response, Steven said, was simply to say, with a slight laugh in his voice, "I didn't know if I should say anything to her or not."

I would later realize he was lying about something or hiding his feelings or true intentions about something anytime he would get that laugh to his voice when he spoke.

Over the course of the next few weeks, I sent Cain a few more messages. He ignored every single one of them. He would then confront Steven and show the messages to him, reportedly saying, "I just didn't want you to think anything was going on,"to him.

"I don't understand why you keep on telling him and showing him the messages," I said to Cain one day. He was sitting on his front porch while I stood in front of him talking. I was clearly upset and told him I needed to speak with him for a moment before I went home.

"He's your husband,"he said with an emphasis on the word "husband."

"But I don't mean anything bad by it,"I replied.

"Are you sure?"he said. He was looking down at his phone. He had that cocky undertone to his voice again.

"I miss you and would love to see you when you return."I sent in yet another message to Cain that would go unanswered. Two minutes later Cain called Steven up on the phone. Cain was on his way to visit his girlfriend.

"She's texting me again," Cain told him.

"Oh really?"Steven said, looking over at me to where I was sitting on the couch.

"Tell her to chill out. I don't have a problem with her. I'll speak to her when I return."He reportedly said. After reporting the contents of my message to Steven, he then hung up the phone.

Whenever Cain returned, he came into the house to apparently examine some of the latest work Steven had done on the flooring.

"Hello, April," he said to me as he walked in through the front door.

"Hello," I shyly and quietly replied to him.

Apparently, he hadn't heard me. He said hello to me one more time as he walked through the hallway examining Steven's work. He then stood by the door talking to Steven as I fumbled around in the kitchen, deciding on a bottle of wine that I would only end up putting back in the cabinet. I avoided his gaze, and he left soon after.

Even though I had avoided Cain when he was at the house earlier that day, I still wanted to talk to him.

"He's down there, just go," Steven said.

I walked down the hill very nervous-like. Cain was there alone. I knocked on the door.

"Come in," he said from the kitchen.

I walked in the door and stood there for a moment. I wasn't sure what to say or where to even begin. He began talking first. He asked me if it was a particular issue about the past that I wanted to understand or know about. *Of course he would know what I wanted to speak with him about,* I thought. He always seemed to know me so well.

He stood up tall and superior like as he talked to me. I burst out in tears when he began to speak. It all just sort of came out. I sat with him for a long time that afternoon speaking with him on the couch. I loved being there with him.

"…And what do you think about me?" he said at one point during our conversation. He tilted his head to the side and looked at me knowingly with that pleased look in his eyes.

I smiled shyly and blushed. "I think you already know what I think about you," I said.

Of course he already knew what I thought about him. He read everything I wrote, even though he would consistently deny it, saying "I don't know what you're talking about,"when I would hint around about him reading my blog.

We kept talking until it started getting late. I wished that I could stay there with him forever, but I knew I had to leave eventually.

"How old are you?" I asked him with curiosity written all over my face. He told me. He then titled his head up with a look that said: *Can you believe it?*

I giggled and looked up at him in amazement. I guess I must have been a bit overbearing as he complained about how warm it was in the house and directed me to come out onto the porch with him.

I followed him outside. "Why do you pay so much attention to me?" I asked him.

"I pay attention to everyone. I like people," he said. He just smiled as if he had no idea the impact that his words had on me. I felt tears welling up in my eyes. He meant the world to me, yet I was apparently just some other person to him.

"I better go home" was all I said in reply.

"Ok, see you later," he said.

I turned around and ran up the hill, unshed tears blurring my vision. When I got home I sent him a message; "I love and admire you, but apparently all I am to you is just some dumb girl."

I then went and found that bottle of wine I had previously placed back into the cabinet. He didn't reply, but the next day he stepped up onto the front porch talking to Steven. They weren't saying anything about me, of that I was fairly certain, but Cain had a very hard and serious expression on his face whenever I looked out the window to see what was happening outside. The next day he left to spend the week with his girlfriend.

Thirteen

$\mathcal{I}$t was true. Being as of yet only in my mid-twenties,

at that point in my life I was, truly, just some dumb girl.
But all that was soon to change.

The next Thursday afternoon I was walking
down the long dirt road to go and meet Hope as she got
off of the school bus. It was a warm day, and the sun was
shining. I was wearing a pair of blue jeans and a crop
top, leaving my midriff bare. Yes, my outfit was a bit
revealing, but I was young and had an amazing figure

that I worked hard every day to maintain. Why not show off a bit?

Joey's dog (Joey was my brother-in-law) was walking down to the end of the dirt road at the same time as I was, so I had this intuition that Cain might be back in town. When I got to the end of the road, I stopped and stood under a shade tree as I waited for Hope.

A moment later Cain pulled in onto the road from the highway. He gave me a slight wave and a polite smile. His eyes then traveled downwards towards my bare stomach. His gaze lingered for a long time until he had to force himself to look away and put his focus back on the road. I didn't smile or wave back, but instead just stared at him. He ignored me at his own will, so why shouldn't I do the same in return back to him?

He continued down the dirt road normally and disappeared around the bend of the road as he made his way home. It wasn't but about a minute later before he came barreling back down the road faster than I had ever seen him drive before. He flew right past me before stopping to turn back onto the highway and disappearing again.

From that day forward I saw him nearly every day, coming down the road at the same time I was walking. Only once before in the two years since Hope had started school had I ever seen him come home at that time. Was it just a coincidence? Perhaps it was just a coincidence, though my instincts told me otherwise. As I would discover in the ensuing months, there would be a lot of coincidences surrounding this man.

Every day that he drove by after that initial day, he would always have the windows rolled up. Sometimes he would be driving and sometimes Joey would be driving, but he would always just cruise right by, as if to make a point that he was too good to talk to me. If I ever wanted to talk to him, he would ignore me and make damn sure I knew it too. But something more was happening. His behavior was starting to do something to me. My thoughts were slowly beginning to focus more closely on *him*.

"You're the closest thing to a father I've ever had," I sent to Cain in yet another message.

He ignored the message and kept driving by as usual every day. When I went out for a walk that very next Saturday after I sent the message, he made a point, when heading to his girlfriend's, to yet again drive right by down the road at the same time I was walking.

This pattern of him continuously driving by me continued for several weeks until one fall evening on a Saturday night when I came down to his house part-drunk.

As I would tell Steven a few weeks later, "You know, I'm not really sure why I went down there. I'm not exactly famous for my good judgment when sober, let alone when I'm drunk!"

I told Steven that evening that I was just going to step outside for a few minutes. I then promptly disappeared down the road until I found myself standing in front of Cain's door. His truck was in the driveway. He was home- alone. The alcohol giving me courage, I knocked on the door.

"Come in," he said. I went in and sat down on the couch. He was not in a good mood. I began to get upset. He told me very harshly to leave and pointed towards the door. He then proceeded to tell me how he found my last message to him to be "creepy."

"You sent me a message saying I was the closest thing to a father you ever had. I found it creepy."

I started to say something, but didn't know what I could say. I was confused inside.

"We've already been through this. You're my daughter-in-law, April; nothing more, nothing less." He had such an asshole tone to his voice.

I began to cry. My tears made him even angrier, and he tried to kick me out again.

"Can I use your bathroom?" I asked.

"Yeah."

I walked into the bathroom. I had to pee, but there was no toilet paper. I walked back out, and he handed me some. I went to pee, straightening out my clothes in the mirror before I came back out.

I gathered my courage up and went to stand beside where he was sitting on the couch.

"I've been shy all my life, but for once I want to be bold," I said to him, still standing.

I then went to sit on the floor beside the couch where he was sitting. I rested my head on the side of the couch as I looked up at him. He said he wanted to be left alone to watch TV. I just kept talking.

"Are you scared of me?" I teased.

He started to open his mouth to say something but quickly caught on to the flirtation behind my words and teasing tone of my voice. He just looked at me, and I continued.

"Are you scared of a girl half your age?" I asked him.

I giggled, nearly falling over. I then asked him if he would ever want to be intimate with me. He looked at me for a minute and then said, "You're married to my son."

"Oh, no, I don't mean right now!" I said, still giggling.

"Hypothetically," He stated. I nodded my head yes.

"I like women my own age," he went on to tell me, without ever answering my question, with a look that proclaimed *I'm full of shit and you and I both know it.* I just stared at him.

Tears began to mix in with laughter as I kept talking to him, alcohol still partially blurring my mind. I wasn't completely drunk, but I was buzzed enough to have some artificial courage to enable me to say enough things to embarrass myself later on.

He then began to insult me. "It's unhealthy," he said of my tears. He then went on to make some small talk with me. He'd try to throw things into the conversation to throw me off guard, a habit I found that he would go on to repeat in the future multiple times. He'd throw in a statement I made in a recent blog posting to confuse me. After all, he always swore up and down that he didn't know what I was talking about. He knew nothing about any "blog."

"I love you and admire you," I said as I looked up at him through my tears.

He calmly nodded his head as he looked at me. He then said,"Why?"

He didn't look fazed or uncomfortable in the slightest by my declaration of love for him, but he did look as though he seriously didn't get it; as if he truly couldn't understand what on earth I saw in him.

This conversation continued on until Steven came driving down the hill with Hope. He was coming to bring me home. I didn't move from the spot where I was at, but just kept sitting beside the couch on the floor and resting my head on the armrest. I could have stayed there all night. In fact, I wanted to.

Steven and hope came through the door a minute later. Hope started playing on the iPad that Cain handed her. She was just being so loud!

I raised my voice slightly at her, saying, "Turn it down!"

"Don't yell at her!" Cain's voice suddenly boomed out, startling me.

I cried out in a very feminine way and fell back onto the floor. I looked up to see Cain looking at me with this look of satisfaction on his face. He had done that on purpose, I was certain of it.

I sat there on the floor just staring up at him, saying nothing. He had my full attention. Steven came and lifted me up off the floor.

I came back over beside Cain. "I have to talk to you," I said.

"Not right now,"Cain said softly, looking at me.

I opened up my black wrapper I was wearing to reveal the long-sleeved crop top I had on underneath, baring my stomach. Cain's eyes darted instantly to my bare stomach as a dark look came over him. He fixed his eyes to my stomach. I kept my wrapper held open slightly with my hands. I gasped and he eventually tore his eyes away.

Recognizing the sexual desire written in his eyes, I gave him a slight smile as though I was flattered. I was accepting of his desire for me. His eyes were still dark and his expression serious when he did finally look up at me and turn back to talk to Steven.

Steven tried to drag me out the door again. Not wanting to go, I allowed myself to fall back to the floor again by Cain's feet. I looked up at him.

"I want to stay with you," I said softly.

He looked at me, partially nodding as if he understood, yet didn't say anything. Eventually, I left with Steven. I went home and sent Cain a message telling him how masculine and wonderful I thought he was.

Two days later he sent a copy of the message to Steven with the big bold words "**From Your Wife**" written at the top of it.

After that weekend Cain never did have a relationship with his long-term girlfriend of nearly a decade ever again, only seeing her on occasion here and there. My life or relationship with Steven wouldn't ever be the same again either.

Cain never actually answered my question that night, the question of whether or not he would ever want to be intimate with me. Never once did he say no, even though he was careful not to say yes either- at least not with his words. His eyes told a different story.

After what had happened, I never went and sent Cain any more messages- not for a long time anyway, and never in an attempt to get a response from him or to get his attention in some way. I was maturing on an emotional level- and a sexual one.

It's hard to describe what was happening, but I felt changes starting to happen within me. I began experiencing things I had never experienced before. My thoughts towards Cain started changing. In the most random of places, such as driving to the grocery store on a routine shopping trip, I would begin to think of Cain. I would start to ache between my legs whenever I thought of him as superior to me. Sometimes it would begin to burn. It would hurt, but I liked it. I tried to tamp it down, tried to understand it, but the thoughts kept coming. I would walk around unfocused. My eyes would glaze over, and a fever would overtake my body.

I was sick- bad sick. I still slept with Steven, but I began to look up and imagine it was Cain lying over me. I began to drink more often. I would sometimes get horny when I would drink then hate Steven for what I considered to be him taking advantage of me in my drunken state whenever I woke up the next day, unable to remember what had happened. I had never had that happen before. I had never felt such feelings. Alcohol had never posed such a danger to me before.

All of Cain's actions even from as early on as the summertime began to put a subtle antagonism between

Steven and I that was growing by the day. Every time Cain would forward a message or call Steven up when I would contact him I would grow just a little further apart from Steven. I began to lose respect for Steven. I even began to resent him. By the end of the year, I would stop sleeping with him entirely.

Fourteen

$\mathcal{T}$wo days later after the incident where I arrived partially drunk at Cain's house, I sat down to write a letter to Cain. Being the shy person that I always was, I was much better at writing than at speaking.

This wasn't the first time I had written a letter to Cain. I had also sat down to pen a letter to both him and Steven several years earlier, whenever Steven had tried to divorce me, in the attempt of explaining how I felt. Cain never answered me then, but that was a long time ago. Surely things had changed after all these years- or so was my way of thinking.

After having penned the letter to Cain, I told Steven that very afternoon that I needed to give Cain the letter.

"Let me see the letter," Steven said to me.

"No. By asking to see the letter, what you are really implying is that you don't trust me."I was a bit over-emotional, but it meant the world to me to tell Cain how I was feeling. Since I couldn't seem to do it in spoken words, I was determined to at least do it through written words.

"Ok." Steven dropped the issue.

I began walking down to Cain's house. I knocked on the door. No answer. I walked back up the hill in tears, believing Cain was ignoring me. Steven told me to calm down. Cain was only in the shower.

I gave it a few minutes and walked back down again. Cain was sitting out on his front porch, putting on his shoes.

"Hey, what are you up to?" he asked me as I approached him.

"I'm not staying. I just came to give this to you." I handed him the letter. "You are the cruelest person I've ever met,"I told him.

"Now why would you say that?"

I shook my head and began walking back up the hill, tears in my eyes. I saw Cain reading my letter as I was walking back home. He appeared to be amused by several parts of it.

Granted, my letter *was* a bit on the dramatic side. It was a full two-and-a-half pages long, and it explained how I felt. I had penned the letter insisting that I didn't view him in any kind of romantic or sexual way. After all, there's no telling what Cain was capable of doing. For all I knew, he would give Steven the letter or even a copy of it. I wrote to him;

> *It is a bit hard to describe what I mean whenever I say that I love you. There are many different ways that one can love another. I'm not really sure what it is, but when I say I love you, I mean that I love you in a non-sexual way. Nobody has ever taken care of me or done so much for me the way that you have. Even though it probably means*

nothing at all to you, it means
the world to me.

I went on to reminisce about the past;

> *...It is only that you*
> *have hurt me so many times*
> *before in the past that I was*
> *scared to come around you.*
> *But do you remember the time*
> *you were there, helping me on*
> *that cold winter's day? It was*
> *with both a mixture of fear*
> *and admiration that I would*
> *look at you. That day changed*
> *everything for me. It made me*
> *feel as though somehow it was*
> *Ok to be around you, as if*
> *everything would be Ok if I*
> *did come around...*

Of course, thinking that Cain would care enough
to give me the time a day was pure wishful thinking on

my part. I couldn't understand. Why was he still ignoring me? So many years had now passed. Didn't that count for something? Did I say something wrong? Did I creep him out or something still?

Cain never shared the contents of my letter with Steven. He came up to the house that afternoon and stood there talking to Steven about something. I was in the laundry room loading the dryer. I could see him through the window as he was talking. Somehow I had this sense that he knew I was watching him.

It was as if he was purposely ignoring me. Standing outside the window where I was working, he sipped on a drink that he held in his hand while he casually spoke with Steven, who was busy fixing a work trailer of his. He reportedly talked about his plans for going out that evening, and how he had plans to go out of town with a few others to the casinos.

How was it that he had all the time in the world to travel around to see others and to have fun, yet somehow he couldn't go five hundred feet out of his way to come and talk to me?

That next weekend Steven was down at the end of the driveway. He had been working on his truck, and Cain had contributed some oil and other things to him. Steven was going to take the truck out for a test-drive to see how it was running. Cain insisted on coming along.

I stood at the top of the driveway watching everything that was happening. Cain strode across the yard towards the truck. Before entering the truck, he turned and gave me a cold, blank stare. He then got in the truck. I continued to stand there. The two then drove off together. I turned around and walked back to the house.

There were instances during the ensuing weeks where Cain would come around and talk with Steven. He didn't ever come inside the house, but would instead be out in the yard speaking with Steven whenever he happened to see him. Sometimes it looked as though he might have made a purposeful trip to go and talk to him, other times he was doing something work-related (the two men often shared tools or used each other's property for work-related purposes).

One chilly evening a little before Thanksgiving I saw Cain outside in the yard. He dumped some items out back and then came up to speak with Steven, who was outside by his truck doing some maintenance on it.

I cracked the door open a bit as I watched all of the happenings from the screen door. Why was he doing this to me? I began to cry. None of it made any sense. He was out there carrying on and having a good time with Steven, even though Steven would later relate back to me that he was largely ignoring Cain.

I slammed the door shut. Through the window, I could see Cain quickly turn around and look in my direction upon hearing the noise. I ran into the bedroom where I threw myself on the bed and began crying my eyes out. I didn't know if I could be heard outside. I didn't care. What did it matter? Never once had he been bothered with me despite all of my confusion, hurt, and pain.

Lying on the floor of the living room one afternoon, listening to old-school rock music and feeling completely depressed, a poem began to run through my mind. As was often the case with me, the thoughts just kept coming, and I knew I had to write about them.

I set to work drafting a blog post, mixing fantasy with reality. It was a dream, telling of the emotional energy of an electric guitar mixed with the soothing baritone of a man's voice. It was anti-feminist prose at its finest, speaking of a man being in charge of a woman and consoling her with his words, while at the same time catering to the male tendency to view their penises as the center of the world.

A soon as I had written that posting, it was almost as if Cain had done a complete flip into being the nice guy again. The very next day, as was oftentimes typical in those days, Steven had asked Cain to watch Hope while we went to the grocery store. Steven wasn't feeling particularly well that evening, so I agreed to drive.

We pulled up in Cain's driveway. I stayed in the car while Steven got out and began to walk up to the front porch with Hope. Instantly Cain came out of the house to meet Steven. He looked over to where I was sitting in the driver's seat with a very pleased look on his face.

I was too shy to look right at him, so I just rested my head against the door, a slight smile on my face, while I waited for Steven to come back to the car. Cain handed Steven a bag filled with some specialty items he had come across on one of his jobs. Steven promptly came back to the car, and we headed to the store.

Cain brought Hope back up to the house after we returned from the store. I busied myself putting away our groceries and other things that we had bought. Steven stood at the front door, barring Cain from entering the house. I refrained from looking over at Cain. He stood and talked with Steven until Steven told him he had to promptly hit the toilet. Steven then shut the door, and Cain left.

Later that evening Steven said to me, "He kept looking right at you, as if he was waiting for you to say something to him."

And he can just keep *waiting*, I thought.

On Thanksgiving Day, Cain showed up unexpectedly at our house. Steven and I were conversing in the kitchen while I cleaned up the mess from the dinner I had just cooked for us. As luck would have it, of course, we were talking about Cain.

"I just don't understand his recent actions. I think it's obvious by now that he's playing some kind of head games with me…But why? I mean, if he was any other man I think the answer would be obvious. But what is it that he wants? I never got the feeling that he disliked me. Actually, I always got this feeling that he cared a lot more than he would ever let on. But I know that someone that truly cares for another doesn't just leave them to cry their eyes out for weeks like that."

"I'm telling you he doesn't know you're that upset,"Steven attempted to reassure me.

"How could he not know? I'm sure he's probably got it marked on his calendar that 'if I just ignore her X amount of time, she'll eventually come running back to me, missing me.' Perhaps those little head-games might work on his girlfriend, but he'll find they won't work so easily on me."

"I don't know what he wanted to manipulate you for, but he was obviously manipulating you for something," Steven said.

Of my text messages to Cain, Steven then said, "You don't say that to your father-in-law! The word 'masculine,' it's kind of…sexual."

"I was drunk! Surely I get a free pass for that?" I said, giving Steven my best pouty face.

"Um, no… Nobody would believe that to be a legitimate excuse…" He wasn't mad at me, only enthusiastic.

"I'm sure he probably thought that I hated him all these years. He probably never knew just how much I truly looked up to him and loved him. I've come to believe that you men truly are clueless. It's like the husband who all of a sudden gets hit with divorce papers. 'But, honey, I thought we were SOOO happy!' You men never do seem to get it. Men don't ever seem to understand whenever a woman is unhappy, or when she actually likes him.

"No, I never truly hated him. I love him to death, and I doubt he will ever understand just how much. It's hard to explain why. In truth, there really is no male equivalent. I looked up to him, as a father-figure perhaps. I don't really know how to explain it. It's difficult. It's not like guys out there routinely go looking up to so-called 'mother figures.' It just doesn't work that way. And as far as the idea that I'm too emotional B.S.? HE'S the one who's making me cry!

"And I tell you," I continued on as I waved a wooden spoon in Steven's face, "I take back anything and everything I ever said about women being like children. It's you MEN that are the real babies. You claim to all be so tough yet somehow you can't handle a few woman tears?"

I was on a roll at this point. "Us women put up with so much crap from you men and are told by society to just 'deal with it' because it's just 'boys being boys.' We even allow you men to impregnate us! So if I get emotional from time to time, then he can just DEAL

WITH IT. That's what us WOMEN do in regards to you MEN! We DEAL WITH IT!"

Steven contemplated my words for a few minutes, and, having no legitimate case against them, gave an expression that said, "Yeah, can't argue with that."He then stepped outside to dump the scraps out for the animals.

As he was coming back in I looked out the open door and saw Cain driving away in his truck. Cain had been out there? My heart skipped a beat.

Steven related to me how he had stepped outside only to turn around and see Cain. "I didn't know he was out there,"he said. "I just turned around, and he was walking up the steps. He saw me and jumped back off the steps real quick. It looked like he almost fell. He asked if we were coming down to my aunt's for Thanksgiving dinner this weekend. He didn't even call beforehand."

I didn't have much more to say. Had Cain heard the things we were saying about him?

Fifteen

$\mathscr{I}$t was only a couple of days later that I found myself without a working car. It was a chilly day, and it was drizzling rain.

When it was time to meet Hope at the bus stop that afternoon, I put on my jacket and boots and took off out the door walking. As I was walking by I noticed both Cain and Joey were home.

As I rounded the corner only about a quarter of the way down the long road, Cain began to drive up behind me. *Breathe, just breathe,* I told myself as I kept walking down the road.

A minute later Cain pulled up and stopped beside me. "Need a ride down to the bus stop?"he said.

"No!" I said quickly- perhaps too quickly. I was still feeling a bit mortified from recent events and still a bit embarrassed over the whole situation.

I remember watching him drive away. My heart pounded so hard in my chest as I wondered if he had gotten out just for me. I suspected that he had, even though I knew he would never say it. Yes, I hoped that he had done it for me, even while at the same time I didn't *want* him to admit it.

I watched him drive on, part of me wanting to know that he had done it all for me yet the other part hoping that he would keep on driving, and pull out onto the highway whenever he reached the end of the dirt road. I'm sure he knew as well as I did that he would only look foolish and lose his status in my eyes if he turned around and came right back home.

He kept driving on to some destination unknown to me. I walked down to the end of the road and waited for the bus to drop Hope off. Hope and I then walked home together. When we got back home I sat by the window, looking out towards Cain's house. Only a few short minutes after we had returned home, he pulled up into his driveway.

I pulled the blinds shut and attempted to distract myself with something- anything- but nothing was working. I laid on the couch and cried until I could cry no more. Nobody could ever know just how much I wanted to accept that ride from him, but I feared what would happen if I did. I didn't want to only ever talk to him whenever it was convenient for HIM. I just couldn't take that ride from him only to have him say God only knew what to me before then dumping me off at the end of the road leaving me feeling even more broken and alone than I had before.

The next time I saw Cain was a few weeks later, at Christmas. It was a family gathering, on Steven's side of the family, and we were all eating Christmas dinner together as we did practically every year.

I was up at the counter getting some food. Cain, who had come alone, attempted to make some small talk with me. Obviously sensing my discomfort, he appeared to be enjoying himself immensely.

"Hello, April," he lightly teased as he attempted to start up a conversation with me. He was standing right in front of me now as I turned away from the food bar. "What have you been up to?" he said.

Even though I didn't respond, I couldn't stop the mortified look that came over my face. Here I was, face to face with him, for the first time since that incident several weeks ago at his house. Thankfully someone else interrupted him a second later to talk to him. I sped away to another part of the room.

Although I did my best to evade him that day, it seemed like he was paying a lot of attention to me. A bit later he was talking with a couple of the guys off in the kitchen. I was sitting a few feet away. I thought I saw him look back at me once as if he was keenly aware of my presence.

Later I got some dessert and sat down at the table. Cain came and sat down to my left, while his brother-in-law took a chair a couple of spots away to my right. We were the only ones at the table, as everyone else had scattered elsewhere around the room.

He attempted to make small talk with me again. I looked up at him this time, my mouth open ready to reply, but before I could get the chance his brother-in-law had cut in saying something. I looked down again to my food, examining it as I took small bites, and quietly listened to their conversation.

About thirty minutes later it was time to open presents. Everybody took a spot off in the main room while I found myself sitting across from Cain yet again. He was still at the table yet had turned his chair around to converse with others in the main room. I was sitting directly in front of him, facing him. He turned to his right to talk with his mother for a while.

While they were engaged in conversation, I lifted my head up to look at Cain. As he turned back, he caught me staring at him. He was so serious, never smiling, as he looked me deep in the eyes. He never wavered; he never broke eye contact with me. It was as if his eyes just held me there, captivated and hypnotized by him. I innocently looked at him for a time before lowering my gaze downward, looking away from him and off to my right.

After a time, still keeping my gaze lowered, I returned my focus back to what was going on with the crowd over in the next room. He kept his focus on me for a few more moments before finally turning away.

Steven and I were fighting again. I was so overly emotional. I felt as though I couldn't breathe. I couldn't even complete an entire workout. I couldn't function normally. The situation was bad and only getting worse. I was growing more miserable every day, having to stay there living right next door to Cain and having to contend with Steven's refusal to see the severity of the situation.

"Please, cut him out of our lives! Don't allow him back up here!" I said, speaking of Cain. I pleaded with Steven to listen, but he only became angry and irrational with me.

"You don't just cut people out of your life! I wasn't raised that way!" he said, raising his voice.

Anger and resentment, quickly turning to hatred, boiled within me. I had already begun to emotionally distance myself from Steven. I would recoil any time he would try to get close to me.

"Don't touch me!" I cried out without thinking one day while I was doing the dishes after he had come up from behind me to wrap his arms around me.

"Are you repulsed by me or something?" he asked me, stepping back a couple of feet.

I didn't reply. Was he blind? Did he not see how I was beginning to cry all the time, drinking myself into oblivion several times a week, all the while asking a million questions about his father and crying over his actions?

I just wanted to be left alone. Steven tried to cheer me up by buying me things I wanted or trying to have fun with me, just like we used to do in the old days, but nothing was working. In fact, his attempts to be closer to me or to help me were only making things consistently worse.

I wanted to leave, but where would I go? I had been dependent on Steven our entire marriage. I had been a quiet, demure housewife, simply devoting all her time to her home and family. Until recently, Steven took center stage in my life; that is until my thoughts began to focus nearly exclusively on Cain.

Cain had suddenly become the other man in our relationship. He had way too much power over my thoughts and emotions. It tore my heart in two how everyone around me seemed to fit effortlessly into Cain's life- everyone except me.

It killed me just a little more inside every time Cain would take my daughter out somewhere or take her to another family event. Everyone had a place in his life, even his ex-wife. Everyone had been places with him, communicated with him or even worked with him while I was left with nothing.

Bringing my daughter home from Christmas dinner at his ex-wife's house a few evenings later, Cain came up to the house. I was sitting on the front porch. I had things in my heart that I needed to say to him. Maybe I could do something to make a relationship with him, to make whatever had gone wrong right again. I at least wanted to try.

Cain walked up to the front porch and asked me a question, regarding us going to another family event in a couple of days. I answered him. I had a pleading look in my eyes as I looked at him, a look he had obviously noticed given his sympathetic expression. But I couldn't form the words to say anything more. He just came up the stairs and walked right past me, following Steven into the house. He never said anything more to me. He never even looked at me again.

I was punished any time I would dare try to communicate with Cain. Every time that I tried to reach out in some way, Cain would start calling Steven up, at which point Steven would confront me about it, and the antagonism between us would grow. Yes, Steven still loved and wanted me, but by that point it was really only Cain that I desired.

Sitting at the bar section of a local restaurant a couple of evenings after Christmas, my heart was officially broken. I had thoughts swirling around in my head that somehow Cain would walk through the door and I would get to live out my fantasy of being with him. Staring at the entrance, I dreamed that Cain would walk through it, smile at me, and come and sit beside me while we talked through the night. I fantasized that somehow he would come for me and that everything would be all right.

It's not like those kinds of fantasies were new to me. I had similar ones all those many years ago after Steven had disappeared on me. The difference was that this time I was hopeless. I had a child. I had no money and no place to go. At least before I had the freedom and the means to leave- but not anymore.

"We've all been there sweetie," the bartender, a woman not much older than myself, told me sympathetically as she placed a free cup of coffee on the bar before me. It's not like I had the money to pay for it.

"Thanks," I said gratefully, barely even touching the warm brew. I had no appetite, but I just couldn't face going back home to the misery and hell that my life had become.

An older gentleman took a seat beside me, ordering a cold beer and some dinner. He wasn't half bad, being tall and in good physical shape still, but he was far too old to really be attractive sexually. He made some small talk with me.

I sat there quietly, smiling up at him. *Would he take me home?* I wondered. Could I find someone else? Was there anyone else out there who might be a companion to me and take away my pain and misery, even if only for the night?

There was a small crowd gathering around the other end of the bar, but nothing looked all that promising. Finally giving up hope, weary and exhausted and feeling as though I was succumbing to illness, I headed back home, back to the very place where I would have once given anything to be- but the place I now regarded as Hell.

The next morning I packed up a bag of my belongings, taking only the necessary things I would need for a few days. Steven wasn't going to listen to me. He was never going to do anything. His head would perpetually stay lodged up his ass where it had pretty much always been. What had I ever seen in him? I had truly been such a dumb little girl when we met.

It was probably only the fact that he had been the first and only guy to take me out and really show any interest in me that I had originally fallen for him. I had been young and naïve, with no mother around, only having Lenard who had never truly cared to prepare me for the world outside. How I hated him now too since I had gotten married. I resented everything he stood for. As my mother had always declared to me growing up, he had truly brainwashed me.

In many ways, I was still young and naïve. As I headed out, I sent Cain a couple of text messages- messages that he would ignore, as always.

When later asked by Steven to send him a copy of the messages, Cain reportedly declared quite gruffly, "I don't pay attention to things that don't matter."

Was I truly expecting anything more from him? I headed to stay across town with my grandparents. How did my life get to such a point? Would there ever be any hope of escape for me?

Steven came and got me later that evening. He stood there in the doorway, looking both gentle and strong. It was true that I was still attracted to him, but I knew my relationship with him would probably never be the same again; at least it would never be the same so long as we stayed there.

"I blocked his number," he told me.

"You promise?"I asked, looking up at him.

"Yes, if he tries to call me it won't go through. I blocked every one of their numbers- all of my family. It's just going to be me, you and Hope now."

I allowed him to hold me, and a little while later I returned home with him.

Sixteen

$\mathcal{L}$ife resumed on as normal after we came back home,

though nothing about my thoughts or feelings had changed much. I tolerated being back, as I had no real choice in the matter. I tried to explain to Cain why I said the things I had said to him. Steven had asked him on the day that I left if he would speak to me if I came down there. A quick and agitated "No!" was his only response, according to Steven. Cain ignored me, the way he always had before.

A few days later, after the New Year had already begun, Steven was working down the hill to fix our driveway. Cain quickly came out, shovel in hand, and started working right beside him.

I had been crying again that day. To relieve some of my hurt and pain, I put on my best belly-dancing outfit,- a beautiful three-layer white skirt with a belt and bra decked out with gold beads and jewels- placed a beautiful white flower in my hair right behind my left ear and began dancing around the living room to my favorite music. I attached the four brass cymbals to my fingers and began playing along with the beat of the drums in the background.

Having been a music lover all my life, dancing was one of my favorite hobbies. I had been belly-dancing for years, having long been captivated by the sound of middle-eastern music. I always loved the sensuality of the dance and the way it seemed designed to move along with and accentuate all the curves and contours of a woman's body without being too overtly or vulgarly sexual. The dance was feminine and graceful, and I delighted in it.

A short time later, I turned off the music and walked outside, still in my dancer's outfit. It was a bit chilly outside, but it wasn't too bad. Steven came back up the hill to get a couple of tools. I played around a bit, walking over to him, shimmying my upper body and flirting around with him.

"Uh-huh," he said when he noticed the deviant smile on my face. He came over and put his jacket over my shoulders.

Though I was attempting to be happy and playful, I looked away from Steven for a minute to where Cain was working down the hill. Tears filled my eyes yet again, and I turned away to look back at Steven.

"You can come down there," Steven said before turning around to walk back down the hill. "Come on."

After zipping up the jacket Steven had given me, I walked down the hill. I sat down on the tailgate of the truck, swinging my legs happily and just watching the two men work. I was always content that way. More than anything else, I loved to just simply hang around while either Steven or Cain was working on something.

Steven was working a little ways away, while Cain kept going back and forth, oftentimes passing in front of me. He acted like his normal, calm self. He seemed happy enough, either oblivious or simply uncaring of the pain I carried around inside of me- the pain I had carried around for so long.

Cain paused for a moment right in front of me. At that moment Joey's girlfriend pulled up at the house, and Joey came out to leave with her. Cain turned around for a moment, commenting nonchalantly on it, then turned back around towards me. He briefly commented on the flower in my hair, smiling slightly as he talked to me. I smiled at him, and he turned away to start working again.

He and Steven were headed towards Cain's shed to get some more equipment to work with. Steven turned around and motioned for me to follow, saying it was Ok, as if Cain didn't mind. I followed them over towards the shed, simply running along behind and smiling. I loved being down there with him and Cain.

I know it's true that I
should never show my hand…
But how could I have
known how much attention I

would garner when at first
this project began?

And so began the little ditty that would be a game changer in all of our lives from there on out.

So now dear reader
without further ado…
Allow me to captivate
your thoughts for a passionate
moment or two…

A few days after I had been down the hill while Steven and Cain were working, I sat down to pen these lines. The words *you'll never see him again if you publish this* kept racing through my head. It seemed so risky to publish it, but it was what was in my heart. I had lived with the fever for so long. It had died down some over the past few weeks, but what I felt inside and my desire for Cain had not changed. It was still as strong as ever, if not stronger.

I would take the risk of publishing my thoughts and turning them into a small poem for the whole world to see. It was pretty much understood at this point, although it was never said out loud, that Cain read everything that I wrote. I had no way of knowing how it would turn out, or how my words would be received.

Unhappiness eating away at my soul, I sat down quietly one evening and wrote,

Oh can't somebody tell me if
I'm just going crazy..?
Did he lure me into a trap or
was it all in my head?
I swear by the gods above I
didn't mean it. It all started
out so innocent.
Whether this is real or all in
my head it's so hard to tell,
but if he did indeed play me he
did it so well.

Continuing on with my writing, I lamented,

In my ignorance I think I did
wrong...
Something I have never
experienced before, inside
there is a feeling so strong...
How could I have known that
there existed such yearning,
that would lead me to find
myself lying here with a fever
burning..?
I pray now that heaven hear
my prayer, if indeed there be a
god out there...
For I know that despite my
age, I have never before
experienced such a feverish
rage...

Oh, but how those words would set off a cascade of events! Instantly the very next day Cain was gone all day, every day- twenty-four hours a day it seemed- every single day of the week! Joey would be gone as well. There was literally never anyone around. Being that the leaves had fallen off of the trees months ago, I could see everything that happened next door. Day or night, he was never there. He didn't come home for lunch like he always used to and he stayed gone all evening.

Being that Steven had blocked the phone number of all of his relatives, Cain could not contact him. Cain reportedly showed up at Steven's work a couple of times, asking him what was wrong with his phone and offering to lend him one, but Steven declined the offer each time.

So it happened about three weeks or so later that Steven had found a brand-new washer and dryer set for us and called up Cain, from my phone, to ask for his help.

Cain didn't answer the phone so later that evening Steven had to go down to his house and ask him, in person, to help him load up the washer and dryer set. Steven told Cain that he had just called him from my phone. Cain apparently just gave a small laugh and said he thought it was just some random person calling him needing work done or something.

I knew he had to be lying, given the many times over the past year he had seen my phone number via the messages I had sent him. The slight laugh to his voice also gave him away, as it had many times before. There was a reason why he wouldn't answer the phone if it was my number- there had to be.

Cain agreed to help Steven, and after Cain had stopped in the barber shop along the way to get a haircut, the two men then set out to get the job done.

Steven was tired whenever they finally got back to our house that evening with the washer and dryer. He insisted on leaving the appliances in the back of the truck for the evening and unloading them the next day. Cain reportedly kept insisting that he would go in and help him that evening, but Steven was just too tired.

Later, upon seeing that it might rain, Steven changed his mind, deciding it might be best just to go ahead and unload the washer and dryer that very evening, at least getting them onto the porch and covered up if nothing else.

He called Cain from my phone again. Standing on the porch, I predicted, "He's not going to answer the phone if he sees it's my number. First, he won't answer simply because he knows it's my number. Second, he's no fool and probably doesn't believe your story about your phone being broken."

My prediction proved correct. Cain wouldn't answer. "It's probably just because he's got his phone back there on the charger,"Steven said.

Steven could think that all he wanted, but in my heart I knew there was an entirely different reason for Cain's refusal to answer the phone.

***

That night as I laid down and closed my eyes sweet dreams and images began to fill my mind…

I open my eyes.
Smoke is all around me. No,
not smoke, steam. It is steam.
Where am I? It appears to be a

garden of sorts- a modern
garden, perhaps. There is a
stone walkway right through
the center of it. Everything is
silent all around me. I am
alone.

The scene flashes
blank before me. I open my
eyes again. I am lying on the
ground, naked. I feel so
vulnerable, and I feel warm-
so very warm. The steam
continues rising all around
me. Someone is coming. Cain.

The scene flashes
blank before my eyes again
and there he stands right
before me. He kneels in front
of me on the ground where I
lay. He is already fully erect. I
relax down, ready to receive
him. I let my legs fall apart as
he comes closer to me…

His breath is hot and heavy on my neck now. He holds the back of my neck in his left hand as he brings his right hand down. He wraps his right arm around my waist then keeps moving his hand lower until he cups my bottom and begins to lift me up towards him. He enters me, and I begin to moan as he keeps filling me, filling me...

I awoke with a start, my eyes suddenly opening. I was confused. Where was I?

As I looked around the dark room, I realized I was still in bed, alone. I had been dreaming, but it felt so real. *He* felt so real. It was as if he had really been there and I could still feel him as though he had really touched me and had been inside of me.

I moved my legs around; daydreaming as I lay there that he was inside of me. I let the fantasy continue to overtake me for a moment, as if the dream had never really ended. Like a whisper into the wind he was.

I lay there for a moment, unmoving. I didn't ever want to leave the warm comfort of the bed. Later I would go on to write about the fantasy, exclaiming;

Last night I had the sweetest
dream
I dreamt that he came to me
And he filled me so completely
He was exactly as I imagined
he would be

I woke up in a daze, eyes
glazed
It all felt so real

For years he knows he's
captivated my thoughts
Passionate feelings of both
love and hate

Delicate beauty in the flower
of youth
Compared to the lines upon
his face
Memories that time can never
erase

Once upon a time it's true
that he took care of me
But I know he's not the same
person that he used to be

He can never be all that I
imagine him to be
No more, no less, he is but a
fantasy

Seventeen

$\mathcal{T}$he next evening Cain waited patiently, biding his
time until he had finished his dinner, before coming up
and helping with the washer and dryer.

I was nervous. I had washed the dishes twice,
making sure there wasn't a single dish left in the sink. I
tried my best to de-clutter everything and make the
house smell as nice as possible. I made the lighting in the
house dimmer, leaving only one single light on in the
living room. I sat down in the kitchen at the table and
attempted to busy myself with a word-search puzzle
while I waited for Cain to show up.

My dream from the night before was still
foremost on my mind. When Cain walked through that
door, would he be able to see through to my thoughts to

know what I had been thinking and dreaming of? He had always seemed to see right through me many times in the past. Again, he did so truly unnerve me.

A short time later Cain pulled up outside. The front door was already open. Steven called for him to come in as he walked up to the house. He then walked swiftly and purposely through the front door with a swagger. He looked so confident and pleased with himself. He handed Hope a large heart-shaped pillow and then looked over at me, his head tilted slightly upwards as he said, "Smells good in here, April. Are you burning a candle or something?"

So self-assured and confident did he appear as he quickly went to work helping to bring our new washer and dryer set into the house. Sitting there at the table, I observed him as he brought the washer in on a dolly. He didn't need any help nor did he struggle any, so capable was he.

Once the men had gotten our new washer and dryer set up in the laundry room, I brought some dirty towels in to test out the new washer. Cain was right beside me as he helped me for a moment. As I was standing right there in the room with him, so close to him, I kept remembering my dream from the night before. Could he know what I had been dreaming of?

After I had loaded up the towels, I went back to the table. I sat there quietly, working on my word-search puzzle and sipping on a soda. I tried to re-arrange my hair, which I had straightened out earlier, to make myself appear as desirable as possible. I put on my black jacket as it was kind of chilly and swished my hair around until my blonde locks fell gracefully into a mess in front of me, traveling onwards to spill down over my breasts.

The two men came back into the main room. I was still sitting there at the table. Steven casually leaned against the wall over to the left side of the room while Cain came and stopped beside the door. Cain turned to face me directly. He stared me down, a deviant smile on his face. I looked up and met his eyes, giving him a gentle smile.

He stared at me for a few moments longer. With a cocky tone to his voice, he then said quietly to me, "See you tomorrow…"

I opened my mouth slightly, saying nothing. I wasn't sure how to reply. He waited a moment then abruptly turned and confidently strode towards the door. He opened the screen door then stopped, placed his hand high up on the glass, then turned back towards me.

"...or anytime," he finished with a come-on tilt up of his head. He then turned and quickly strode out the door, never once looking back.

Steven gave me a look that said "there you go" at Cain's invitation to come around "anytime," obviously missing the sexual undertones of Cain's voice. It even took me a few moments after Cain had left before I realized what he had really meant.

"He was giving you the stare down!" Steven said to me later after Cain had gone.

I found myself blushing inwardly. Cain had presented himself so well to me. He had been so bold. He had truly charmed my heart. Months later, after all of the drama and heartbreak that I would endure, I would go on to write about that night;

I never asked where
he went or what he did. I
never even cared. I remember

it so distinctly the way his
bad-boy game charmed me
and melted away my heart.
And I remember so well that
night so long ago the way he
put his hand up high on the
screen, and how when he
walked out that door, how he
took with him my heart.

God only knows what might have been had I come to him that next day- but I never did. I tossed and turned all night, managing only to get a whole two hours of sleep. I remembered his words; I remembered his presence there earlier that evening.

The next day he was outside of our house whenever I left to pick up Hope from the bus stop. He looked very focused, quickly unloading the items from the back of his truck. Joey was there working with him.

Cain turned around for a moment and gave me a quick wave, then quickly turned back to his work. Too tired for walking, I got into the car and drove down to the bus stop.

I picked up Hope then drove back home. Joey was leaving, which was typical of him, so only Cain remained behind down at his house. He stayed there, never leaving, for the rest of the day and on into the evening.

Nobody could ever know what a temptation it was to go down there to him, but after all this time and after everything he had done to me (I hadn't even seen him in about a month, after all, and he had yet to answer a single text of mine or bother to communicate with me), he could wait a bit longer. I was not going to let him pull his little disappearing acts on me and then go meet him on a whim to have some illicit liaison with him or something.

Steven had treated me that way when we were younger, but I was a teenager then. No longer was I a teenager, but a woman grown who was coming into her own personality and maturing emotionally more fully every day. I didn't want Cain to see me as just another easy lay. I loved him. I would have never even considered the possibility of sex with him if I didn't, and I wasn't going to fool around casually with him and downgrade my status in his eyes.

What kind of a relationship could I ever hope to have with him then? I would only become someone he was casually sleeping with. He might have the time of his life only to get bored with me a while later, all while I was falling even deeper in love with him.

No, there would never be any chance that I could ever truly be with him then- especially if he ever thought I would just easily jump into bed with a man. If I would so easily do it with him, might he believe I'd also do it so easily with another?

I had to make him wait on the sex. The thought of casually having sex with him- or any man- was so repulsive to me and weighed down heavily on my heart. Yes, I wanted him, but physically desiring him could only ever be the half of my fulfillment. The other half could only ever come from loving him- and in knowing that he could love me in return.

*Because when I feel, I
feel so deeply. When I love, I
love so truly… Inside and out
I am female, I am feminine, I
am woman… Only if I am
sure, only if I can see that he
is real, can I ever open up,
willing and ready, to receive
masculine hardness deep into
the depths of feminine
softness…*

After that day both he and Joey went back to
being gone 24/7. Three days later, however, I saw Cain
come home alone sometime around noon. I went down
the hill to check the mail then walked over to where he
had pulled his truck around the back of his house. He
started to drive back out from around the back of his

house but stopped and rolled his window down whenever he saw me.

"Hey what are you up to?" he said to me in a light, possibly even a bit nervous, voice. He then quickly looked down to where I held a letter in my hand that I had just pulled out of the mailbox. Before I could respond to him, he said, "Oh, checking the mail?"

It was almost as if he was expecting something else. He seemed so clueless, reinforcing my belief that *all* men were truly clueless. I just cocked my head to the side and smiled at him while I nodded.

"Well, got to get back to work,"he said.

I smiled then turned around to walk off. I looked back a couple of times. Once whenever I looked back, I thought I had caught him eyeing me, looking a bit excited. I just shook my head and kept walking up the hill, towards home. Yes, all men really were that clueless.

He parked his truck and stayed there at his house alone for the rest of the afternoon. After that day he returned to his normal routine of being gone 24/7 once again.

214

That next Sunday, sometime in the afternoon, I saw him pull up alone at his house. I walked down the hill. I then walked up to his porch, needing to talk to him, but noticed everything was dark and quiet inside the house. I knocked on the door. No answer.

I headed back up the hill for a few moments before deciding, determined that I needed to talk to him, to go back down and try to knock on the door again. It was still dark and quiet inside the house, with no sign of any movement from within. I knocked again and waited… still no answer. I felt this weird vibe go through me.

I stood on the porch for a few minutes before finally giving up and walking back up to the house. A few minutes later Cain's truck pulled out of the driveway. I felt as though I was being played.

When I got back home, Steven said to me, in a non-accusatory tone, "Where you just down at my dad's?"

I only got annoyed at him, brushing aside his question and walking away. Steven was losing his hold on me more and more every day.

It couldn't have been more than a week or two later that Cain and Joey were at home in the afternoon. Hope was excited to see her grandfather at home, so I allowed her to go down and play. A few minutes later I walked down to Cain's house to go and check on her.

The door was open, and Joey was standing there in the living room, on the other side of the sofa, facing me.

As I walked up to the door, Joey said something to me, but I couldn't understand him. He had spoken so quietly. Confused, I looked at him and said, "What?"

"He's in the shower, and I don't want to be around you- so bye," he said. He had said it so quietly, yet so cruelly, dismissing me with a mere wave of his hand while he continued to stand there.

I walked out onto the porch and sat down in a chair outside. Tears were beginning to form in my eyes. I wouldn't leave the property unless Cain asked me to. I did like Joey and his cruelness cut me. But he was oftentimes like that to everyone anyway.

A few minutes later Steven came driving down the driveway, coming home from work. He stopped on the dirt road, and I walked over to him, riding back with him up to the house. Hope was still down at Cain's, eating.

We pulled up in the driveway and, with tears in my eyes, I told Steven what Joey had said to me.

Steven called Cain a few minutes later, asking if he would help him load and bring a small storage building up to the house. Cain consented to help.

I went back down to Cain's house with Steven. Joey left and I stayed inside of Cain's house with Hope while the two men were gone.

I looked around the house. It's like I could feel Cain's presence. Something inside of me was calm, being there in his house. I felt the familiar warmth and ache begin down below when I thought about how it was *his* house that I was in. Joey had left. Did he really have authority there? *Surely not*, I thought as I relaxed there on the couch- *Cain's* couch.

The two men came back a short time later, after they had unloaded the small structure up at our house. Stepping out the back glass to the back of the house, Steven and Cain were out there together. Cain was talking and smiled as he looked at me. He seemed to be his normal self, if not a bit nervous- or something. I couldn't really understand it, but there did seem to be something off about him that day.

Later Steven related to me how he had told Cain, when they were alone in the truck together, what Joey had said to me. Steven said that Cain's only reply was to look down at his phone, ignoring him completely.

"There's something weird going on," Steven said to me that evening.

Eighteen

$\mathcal{I}$ cannot describe the hurt and pain that I had

suffered, and still there was so much more pain to come.

It was only about three weeks after that evening Cain had been up at the house that I finally sat down and officially published my dream where I was with Cain in the garden.

Mixing my own words in between quotes from the Song of Solomon in the Bible and an infamous old-school bodice ripper romance novel, I turned the posting into my own lyrical masterpiece.

It was as if instantaneously Cain stopped being gone 24/7 and instead would spend his time at home in the evenings.

Early one morning a couple of days later, as I was driving up the driveway coming back home from the bus-stop, I looked over and noticed Cain standing beside his truck. He was standing with his back towards me. I felt this weird vibe. It's hard to explain exactly what it felt like for me, but it was as if somehow he had this superior aura surrounding him, as if he was radiating masculinity. I felt as though, if I could have only seen his face, that he would have been wearing that same smile that he always put on, that half-smile of his accompanied by a squinting of his eyes that he wore whenever things were going his way, or that he wore whenever he believed he was successfully manipulating me to do his bidding.

Of course, I had no way of knowing for sure if he was indeed wearing that same smile or had that same look in his eyes. It was just a vibe I felt.

Though he was never gone day and night ever again, he did take a curious trip up to visit his girlfriend that weekend. I knew that he hadn't seen her in months, and I suspected that the real reason for his trip was probably due to a need for sexual release after what I had written on my blog. Of course, I have no way of knowing this for sure. Perhaps it was yet just another coincidence out of many.

That same weekend, I went down to Steven's grandparent's house for Sunday dinner. I went down there occasionally, taking Hope with me, and I knew there were times Cain went as well- though not all of the time.

Being curious and nosy, Steven called up Cain on the phone to ask if he was going to be there.

"He didn't want to talk," Steven exclaimed matter-of-factly after hanging up the phone.

Steven said that Cain mentioned something about there being a cake down at Steven's grandparent's house. Though I knew it was Cain's birthday in only a couple of weeks, to this day I have never been very clear on whether or not that cake was meant for him or not.

There were a few relatives of Steven's about that afternoon for Sunday dinner. Cain's sister had mentioned, when explaining where Cain was, that he was visiting his girlfriend. The way she had said it...*was everyone expecting him*?

I sat there, feeling a slight blush creep up onto my face. Could it be possible that Cain was out with another woman, all the while thinking of me?

That very same weekend, while Cain was gone, the three of us took shelter in Cain's house when a tornado warning was upon us yet again. Joey was home with three of his buddies. They were playing video games. This time, however, Joey didn't say anything bad to me. He even came up to the house later to get some old games that Steven had. I smiled at him and let him in the door.

My feminine mind wished to believe that Joey was being so nice because Cain had forbidden him to kick me out or be so harsh with me, but perhaps it was simply because Steven was there. In truth, Joey wasn't really nice. He mainly just ignored me, but him ignoring me was, at least, a step above kicking me out of the house. He even, according to Steven, made a slight compliment about me that weekend. Well, as big of a "compliment" as one could expect from him, which wasn't saying much…

Though I did want it to be true that Cain might protect me from him, that he might have actually given a damn and truly cared for me, I simply did not have the evidence one way or another to support such a conclusion. I knew that in the past he had taken care of me and said not to worry about Joey any- but I also knew that Cain was truly not the same person that he used to be.

The next weekend Cain didn't go to his girlfriend's house again. Instead, he went to Sunday dinner. Though Hope and I left the house around time for Sunday dinner, we didn't go down to Steven's grandparents again. Instead, we simply went grocery shopping.

Cain was at home whenever we left the house to go to the store, but he left shortly thereafter, going down to eat Sunday dinner. Though I couldn't prove it, I had the feeling that he went mainly to get into contact with me, given what I had written in my latest blog posting.

Later that afternoon, Cain came out of the house whenever Steven was parked at the end of the driveway. I watched out the window while Cain strode across the yard, handing Steven a decorated cup for Hope. He then turned to walk back to the house as if he didn't wish to stay and talk to Steven.

A few evenings later UPS arrived later than was customary, delivering a package meant for us down to Cain's house. I saw the entire interaction from the window where I was standing, yet again, watching the happenings outside.

Cain was moving things around and putting boxes out on his front porch. I don't know what he was up to, really, but neither did I care. He looked very busy.

He set the package down on a chair outside on the front porch and continued doing whatever it was that he was doing.

Cursing the idiocy of the UPS driver, Steven then jumped in the car to drive down to Cain's house to get our package. As soon as he pulled up in Cain's driveway, as close to the house as he could get, Cain started walking into the house, acting as though he didn't even see Steven.

Steven reported how he called out to Cain, finally forcing Cain to acknowledge his presence. I knew it was practically impossible for Cain not to have seen Steven. It was dark, and Steven had his bright lights on the entire time as he was driving down there.

Though everything happening was very odd and strange, I knew that Cain's actions were never a result of him being weirded out or anything by my love for him. In fact, it always seemed like my love and desire for him pleased him greatly.

In some ways I always felt that he did everything just to get at me- his being gone all the time, his showing up at Sunday dinner and all the other small happenings. But it just didn't make any sense to me.

A few days later, shortly after noon, I had some errands to run. It was a bit chilly outside, and the rain had been coming down all day. I noticed, whenever I stepped into the car to go to the store, that Cain was working on the driveway.

I passed right by him as I was driving. There he was, standing off to the side of the road, the rain gently coming down on him. He paused and leaned casually against his shovel as I drove by, giving me a smile that was part amusement, part approval, almost as if he was trying to say "hey!" to me.

I was wearing my glasses with my hair done à la Ariana Grande. I turned to look at him, raising my eyebrows. I had barely managed to turn back around to put my eyes back on the road, however, before I started smiling and blushing profusely. I continued driving down the road, still smiling like a woman in love. I smiled for the rest of the day.

Later that afternoon, Cain called Steven up on the phone asking a ridiculous question about his truck that practically anyone could have known the answer to. Steven told him to check the issue himself and promptly hung up the phone on him. Another coincidence, I'm sure.

Even though Cain never stayed gone all of the time anymore, I still felt the hurt and pain of never belonging in his life. The sadness just continued. He was always home, but as usual, I was never even worth so much as him walking up the hill for.

How could he gift me with things and why would he go so far out of his way to try to get at me via every third party around instead of just walking up that hill to me? I was right there, wanting him, desiring him and waiting for him to make a move. What was wrong with him? What was he waiting for? Why would he drive so far to visit his girlfriend when all he had to do was come for me- when all I ever required was that he be real and love me?

All I had ever been waiting for was for him to show me that he could communicate with me and make a relationship with me. But apparently, in his eyes, I just wasn't worth it. So many strange things had been going on. Not only did he not have a relationship with his girlfriend anymore, but I also knew that he didn't have a relationship of any sort with Steven anymore either.

And, no, the irony of the situation did not escape me. Yes, I knew that I was a married woman, but a piece of paper and a few vows spoken didn't change what I felt inside and what I felt within my heart. I loved Steven. Not only did he take care of me, but we had shared so many years together, and he was my best friend. I didn't want to hurt him. I didn't mean him any harm nor did I wish to make a fool out of him, but with every passing day, my feelings for Cain just kept growing. It wouldn't be long before I was full blown head over heels in love with Cain, acting irrationally and throwing all caution to the wind and questioning everything I had ever believed in.

Nineteen

What I ask myself
inside is this: If I give him my
body, would he then rip out
my heart?

And so I began to write yet another posting on my

blog, speaking of sex, love and the differences between men and women and how a man should be the one to pursue the woman if he really cares about her. I had been home heartbroken for weeks. If he did indeed want me, why would he not then come for me? Again, he was always there.

The next day Cain was at home all day long, which was an extremely unusual thing for him. I remember the next day, a chilly yet sunny Saturday, how he was working outside all day long in plain sight. He adopted that same stance that he would normally get whenever interacting with me; a dominant stance where he would pull himself up straight to his full height and spread his feet apart as he stood.

I remember looking out the window, noticing him outside working and thinking how magnificent he looked. He looked so strong and masculine, outside working wearing his tan work overalls. He wore no hat on his head that day. I felt like I could die as I discreetly observed him throughout the day.

Everything he did just made me more and more attracted to him. He had his tailgate down, and he would stand there, confident and tall, working out the back of his truck. He would also work on something (a motor perhaps?), on the porch while he would crouch down before it.

As we were leaving to go to the store that very same afternoon, Steven and I were arguing. I wanted to go to the store without him, as I didn't want to be around him and was angry with him. He stopped me before I could leave to go to the store by myself.

"You won't be able to get any groceries without money!" he said to me. He then commanded me to get over in the passenger's seat. "Scoot over!"

I walked around to the passenger side of the car and got in. I was not happy. I felt like I had oftentimes as a child, forced to comply with the wishes of my parents, having no other option or place to go. I felt miserable and trapped. I knew I shouldn't feel that way. I mean, Steven did provide well for me. I didn't have to worry about anything. What right did I have to complain?

As we pulled out of the driveway, Cain turned around to look in our direction (to see if I was in the car, perhaps?). Oh, it would be pure heaven, I thought as we drove off, to run towards him and allow him to hold me in his arms. I could spend the day with him in bliss… If only I could.

"You'll never guess who called me," Steven said with calm amazement as he walked through the door a couple of days later.

He proceeded to tell me how it was Cain who had called him, offering him a hundred dollars for what Steven perceived to be about ten minutes worth of work, to fix something on his truck. He then told me that he went down to Cain's house, but Cain had changed his mind and was able to fix the truck by himself.

That very same afternoon Steven's grandparents came down to Cain's house with clothes and other things they had bought for Hope. Hope went down to Cain's house. Cain then brought her home later that evening.

Cain walked straight through the front door, confidently and with a purpose. I was sitting in front of the television wrapped up in a blanket, watching music videos. I paused the television when he came through the door, but I was so shy I couldn't look his way. He stood there right behind me talking to Steven. Out of the corner of my eye, I could tell that he was looking at me. He had that same cocky tone to his voice, the same cocky tone he always got whenever he was up to something.

Yes, I had long ago begun to notice all the various quirks about him and had observed his behavior patterns often enough by that time. I felt I knew him quite well- at least in some ways. I stayed curled up there on the couch, smiling and blushing slightly, unable to do anything but look vaguely in his direction. I couldn't bring myself to look right at him!

Out of the corner of my eye, I could see that same cocky smile on his face. He was talking to Steven, yet he was still focused on me. I had the gut feeling inside of me that the events of the last few days were about him trying to get to me. He then left a couple of minutes later. I stayed there, still curled up on the couch, smiling.

Whether right or wrong, for better or worse, the heart wants what it wants. It cannot be helped, it cannot be stopped, and reason rarely plays a role in what it so desires. But no matter how much it hurts, loving another does not mean that they will ever love you back in return.

On Easter Sunday a few days later, Hope and I traveled down to Steven's grandparents for Sunday lunch. There was only to be a small gathering there that day, consisting of no more than Cain and his youngest son, me, Hope and Steven's grandparents.

I knew and hoped in my heart all that day before I set out that Cain would be there. I fixed my hair and makeup real pretty that morning and put on my favorite minidress- a flirty and feminine floral patterned white dress with spaghetti straps. It was a very short dress. I certainly couldn't get away with bending over in it without showing everything I had. I thought it showed off my legs well.

Steven made a comment to me before I left that his father and brother might be there. He didn't want me to wear the dress. I got angry and told him that there was absolutely nothing wrong with the dress. I was going to wear it anyway- no matter what he said.

"Alright, whatever," was his only response to me. He wasn't tagging along with us; Hope and I were going alone. As awful as it might sound, that's just how I wanted it. I wanted to be around Cain.

I arrived with Hope a bit early for dinner that day. Cain was not there yet. Betty was in the kitchen cooking still. There was nothing for me to do, so I made my way outside on the porch to sit down and read a book.

It was only a few minutes later that I looked down the hill to see Cain's truck. My heart beat a little faster. I could see him way down the hill, working at the house next door, dragging out materials and who knows what else. It's not like I really cared what he was doing. I was just focused on the fact that he was in the area.

A bit later he began to drive up the driveway. I was still sitting outside on the porch. He then began to turn around and back his truck up on the far end of the yard. I continued to read my book. I heard a strange noise and looked up. Did he slide on a rock or something? No, he had backed up into a tree. He must have been distracted. Was it because of me? Had I distracted him or made him nervous somehow?

He parked and got out of his truck. He started walking towards the house. He stopped halfway across the yard, looked over at me, and then down at his phone for a minute. He then continued walking towards the house.

He went inside, and I heard him talking, saying something to Betty. He was talking about getting some materials out of the house next door or something. I didn't hear the entire conversation, not that I was really all that concerned anyway.

I came inside and sat down on the couch. He started walking towards the bathroom, stopping midways to come closer, but never too close, to where I was sitting on the couch. "Hi, April," he said to me with a knowing smile on his face. He then strode on towards the bathroom.

Cain then left a few minutes afterward to go and get his youngest son. The two men would return later, after what seemed like an indeterminable amount of time.

In the meantime, Hope and I ventured outside. We walked around for a few, observing and handing treats out to the horses next door. I tried my best not to cry. My makeup was perfect and I didn't want to ruin it. *He's coming right back. He really came here for you*, I kept telling myself.

My heart had been so broken for all of those months, and now Cain was finally there, pursuing me, just as I had written on my blog that any man who cared about and was interested in a woman should do.

A man that wants
you and cares will pursue
you. If he can't initiate, if he
can't be the pursuer, then he
either isn't all that interested
or simply doesn't care
enough. It doesn't matter how
much it hurts. A woman
must always be alert to a
man's true intentions and
filter out the men that care vs
the men that only want sex
from her.

A short while later Hope and I walked back to the house. "Those boys better hurry up before their dinner gets cold," Betty said. I giggled inwardly. Indeed, what was taking them so long?

237

After what seemed like an eternity later, Cain and his son finally showed back up. They were in his son's car.

They came inside, and we all sat at the table to eat. Cain sat at the head of the table and placed me off to his right. It felt right and natural, like it put him in charge of everything. He played his part well. I just watched him, fascinated by him. He had the perfect calm, relaxed, yet semi-aloof attitude about him as he sat, casually draping his arm over the back of the chair while he talked and listened to the conversation going on around him. He played the part of courting a woman real well with his actions and attitude. Everything he did was so perfect.

All of a sudden I felt a bit lost. Cain's presence, however, was calming to me. I just watched and responded to him. I kept looking towards him, waiting for him to lead the way and show me what I was supposed to do. I watched and followed his lead on everything. Somewhere in the conversation he turned to me, talking about getting Hope a guitar for her birthday.

"Would you like another guitar, April?" he said as he winked at me. I smiled at him and lowered my head slightly, blushing.

Of course, he never got Hope a guitar for her birthday. I believe he only said that as a way of showing me that he cared about me. By talking about getting a guitar for Hope, he could then casually bring up the guitar he had previously gifted me with a couple of years earlier. He made me feel special.

A minute later I heard my phone going off. It was in my purse across the room. I walked over to the desk that I had set my purse on. Reaching in my purse, I took out my phone and looked at it. When I looked back, Cain was still sitting there at the table, still relaxed and aloof with his arm draped casually over the back of the chair. He was still listening to the talk around him at the table, nodding slightly here and there, yet he was completely zoned out, focused on my legs, his eyes appearing to be glazed over with unmasked desire.

I found it sexually affirmative that he held such desire for me in his eyes. Seeing that he was a hot-blooded male who could completely lose his train of thought over me, I only desired him all the more in return.

After a little while, everyone got up from the table. Cain went into the kitchen to quickly wash the dishes. As there was no dishwasher, everyone generally took turns washing dishes at family gatherings.

I sat there on a stool by the countertop, silently observing him. Even doing the dishes, he managed to retain that same masculine aura about him. He would stand up straight and adopt that same dominant stance of his while he worked. Sitting there observing him, I don't think I had ever realized before that day just how tall he really was. He was certainly a few inches taller than I was.

A bit later we made our way outdoors and began to hunt Easter eggs with Hope. Cain lagged behind indoors. I kept looking for him, wondering where he was. To my mind, it was like a big mystery where he had gone. He was completely charming me. I didn't believe he really had anything all that important to do inside. I figured he was lagging behind so as not to appear eager, thus increasing his value in my eyes.

He walked out the door a bit later, casually wielding a toothpick in his mouth and checking out an old car Betty was trying to get rid of. I was quite positive he had absolutely no interest in the car, yet he would walk around it anyway, opening doors and casually looking about inside of it. I could barely contain the excitement he was building within me- not necessarily a sexual excitement, but the kind of excitement a girl gets when a charming man is pursuing her- the kind of excitement that makes a girl want to squeal with delight, that makes her heart boil over inside. That's what he did to me that day.

After he was done looking at the old car, he then casually walked and got his drink out of his son's car. I was standing on the porch by that time. I draped my black wrapper over my shoulders in a very graceful and feminine manner, as it was a bit chilly out.

Out of the corner of my eye, I could see him walking. He stopped to stand off to my left, facing right in my direction. He was still quite a distance away. I turned my head to look in his direction. He squinted his eyes and focused on me as if he was pleased that he was getting his way again. He turned his drink up as he continued to look at me.

Slowly but surely Cain made his way up to the porch. He casually leaned against the wall and talked with the others. Hope and I were standing there a couple of feet away from him. He was fixing to leave with his son in a minute. They were going out to the casinos, he told us.

He rubbed the top of Hope's head. "See you later," he said to her.Then quieter, still talking to her but mostly directing his words in my direction, he said in a light tone, "…or in a few hours."

Hope and I stayed for a little while longer after they left. I went home that afternoon wondering and waiting. Lenard and his girlfriend showed up with some Easter gifts and other things after we got back, mostly things for Hope.

I kept watching the clock. It was growing later. I didn't understand. What had Cain meant? Would he be up there later or something? I was confused.

It was only later on that evening that the realization hit me that he must have wanted us to come down there...

Twenty

$\mathcal{I}$ did come down to Cain's house the next day. I

walked Hope next door to play with her friends for a

while. On the way back I started walking towards Cain's

house.

I came up to the front porch then knocked on his

door. "Come in,"he replied from inside.

I walked through the door. He was busy on his

iPad, mapping out the work he had to do and making

some estimates. He made normal conversation with me

and I talked to him for a while. He had been doing some

work over the past few weeks at a local youth center.

"I tell you what," he said with that same cocky

undertone to his voice. He kept his focus on the iPad he

was holding in his hand, never once looking up at me as

he spoke. "They still owe me money. I could see if they would be willing to make a deal to let Hope come up there and play this summer in exchange for the money they owe me," he said.

"Ok, I'll talk to Steven about it."

He said ok, but something just felt off about the situation. The words *I shouldn't be here* just kept ringing through my consciousness.

I got out my phone and started reading a book while he was working. The house was so quiet. He then got up and made a work-related phone call.

He walked over to the wall where his phone was plugged in, charging, and picked it up. He stood up tall and relaxed and leaned against the television while he talked. I sat politely on the couch as he talked business. I noted once again how tall he was.

After he was done talking on the phone, he walked outside to work on something. I followed him. He attempted to make conversation with me again.

"I had to attend a funeral the other day; buried a classmate. He died of diabetes- didn't take care of himself,"he began.

I just silently nodded as I observed him. It was so odd in my mind that this man who had been such an asshole and treated me so terribly over the past year could just all of a sudden morph right back into being his old self again. I had truly missed the way he used to be, but how could he act so normally as if nothing had been going on for the past year- as though nothing was silently happening now between us?

Figuring that Steven would be coming home at any time, I silently slipped away into the house and made my way back up the hill towards home.

I walked back down a bit later to get Hope from next door. On my way back down the hill, I saw Cain move the blinds apart slightly in order to look out the window. He then came out of the house and walked towards us.

I walked up, holding Hope's hand in mine. Without even thinking, I batted my eyes flirtatiously at him. I hadn't even realized what I had done until it was too late- but he did. He had caught it. He looked at me with that smile of his. Oh, he was amused by it!

He handed Hope a lollipop as he looked at me. It was a silent exchange between the two of us. I smiled at him, silently signaling to him that I was ok; that I wasn't hurt or upset in any way. A moment later, Hope and I continued walking back up the hill, towards home. Cain went back inside his house.

> *A man that cares will go out of his way to find out what is wrong if he knows you are hurting. A man who cares would not ignore a woman for weeks or months and leave her to cry her heart out. A man that cares will go out of his way for you and he wouldn't need any excuses to do so… To the extent that he doesn't reach out, is the extent that he simply doesn't care.*

Days went by. I hoped within my heart that he would get in touch with me. Sometimes I would mindlessly gaze down at my phone, wondering why he would never call nor message me. Every time my phone went off I hoped that it would be him, even though I knew deep down inside that it never would be.

Though he was never gone day and night again like he had been at the beginning of the year, he would often leave in the evenings. It was depressing, as I wished that I could sometimes go with him to wherever it was that he went. I wished that I could go *anywhere* with him.

I was in despair again. Hurt so badly from all the things he had done to me and all of the ways he had treated me, I really felt that I needed to talk to him and tell him how I was just too badly hurt and just didn't know anymore about everything regarding him.

About a week or so later Hope and I casually walked down the road, playing together a bit along the way. Cain was at home. He was alone, and his front door was open. Would he not call out to me? Initiate conversation with me somehow? Anything? Years ago he had done so.

Hope and I slowly walked across the yard and up to his front door. He was inside and told us to come in.

We walked in the house. He was friendly and relaxed, simply sitting on the couch. He tried to make conversation with me, but it just wasn't going well. I felt somehow that he was being fake.

Right before we were ready to head home, he got up and got Hope some popsicles out of the freezer. I tried to say something to him, tried to find the right words to say that would explain what was in my heart, but no words would come out.

He relaxed and smiled at me. "You can just come on back anytime you need some more popsicles," he said to Hope as we walked out the door.

I stopped on Cain's front porch. "Go ahead and head up the hill, I'll be there in a minute," I told Hope.

I stood there for a minute then turned back around. Cain was busy talking to someone on the phone- a woman, I thought. He was paying absolutely no mind to me. I didn't know whether or not he even noticed me, or noticed the pain written across my face, or whether or not he even cared.

I could feel my heart inside as if it was slowly dying. I looked over at him then walked to the other end of the porch to give him some privacy. I stood waiting for him to finish his call, but when I came back around to the door a couple of minutes later he had disappeared off into the back of the house somewhere. I walked back up the hill with a heavy heart.

I sat there in the living room for a few minutes before determining that I had to talk to him. I couldn't put it off any longer.

I got up and walked out the door, heading down the hill once again. Halfway down the hill, I stopped. Cain's truck was no longer in his driveway. He was gone- again.

Since I had no other way to communicate with him, I went home and drafted up a text message to send to him:

I was coming to tell you something but you were busy, so I'll say it this way. I'm sure you'll forward or ignore it, but I don't

care because it doesn't matter. I really loved
you and wanted to be a part of your life, but
I've spent nearly a year now in severe pain on
account of how you've treated me. I just
wanted to hear it from you that I could come
around again last summer because I missed
you but you turned your nose up at me and
ignored me. I tried to reach out last June. It's
now April. As you said, I'm just some girl
that married your son, and that's all I'll ever
be. I'm done trying to be a part of your life
because I know I never will be and you'll just
keep hurting me. But you'll always be special
to me.

> *-April*

Cain ignored my message to him, as usual. The
next week was heart-wrenching for me as I tried to
occupy myself. My menstrual cycle came along and
added physical pain on top of the emotional pain I was
already feeling. I watched as Joey and Cain went about
their lives, with Cain never once bothering to concern
himself with me.

"Don't pay any mind to them," Steven told me. But it didn't matter. There was nothing he could do to console me anymore. He bought my favorite cocktails for me, rented movies I liked and tried to be there for me- but it didn't matter. I was already long gone to him, long gone to everyone.

That next Monday Cain called Steven up asking if he wanted some materials he had come across. Cain came up to the house to give the materials to Steven. Steven later recounted to me how Cain was in a hurry to leave. Steven said it was "strange."

Things were only to get much worse from there. The next Friday, I believe it was, as I was driving by to pick up Hope from the bus-stop, I saw Cain outside working on his truck.

I had been drinking earlier that week, attempting to drown out my sorrows, when thoughts came racing to my mind that perhaps I had said everything wrong. Last summer he had told me, "I just wanted you to come to me."

Perhaps if I just did what he said, everything would be ok. If he really did want or love me and would give me shelter then, yes, I was willing to come to him.

I was full-blown infatuated by that point, already beginning to experience the "high" from the increase of various hormones in the body and chemicals in the brain as a result of having fallen in love. I was no longer thinking clearly.

I came back home, barely even making it over the threshold of our front door. "I've got to go see grandpa for a minute," I hurriedly said to Hope.

I took off at a run down the hill, finally arriving to stand in the middle of Cain's yard all disheveled. I hadn't even taken notice of my appearance.

Cain wasn't outside anymore. I looked back and saw Joey slowly driving down the driveway, making his way towards the house. Hope had followed me down the hill. I continued to stand there in the yard, looking around.

A minute later Cain walked out the front door, wiping his hands off with a rag. *Dear God*, I thought, as he appeared to my love-struck eyes like a Greek god of sorts.

I noted the way he held the rag in his hands and took in his appearance. He looked so rough and masculine, walking out in the t-shirt and jeans that he was wearing- clothes still dirty and stained from the mechanic work he had been doing.

He looked at me briefly then looked away. He quickly looked back again, doing a double-take of sorts, as he clearly caught the look of love and infatuation in my eyes and took in my disheveled appearance. He did not look happy. He appeared angry- which only increased my desire for him.

Joey pulled up in the driveway right next to where I was standing. Cain then strode quickly and purposefully towards the car, saying in a terse voice as he went past me, "Don't let her get near the truck." He then got in the passenger seat of the car with Joey and the two of them drove away together.

I stood there for a moment, then turned around to slowly walk back home, Hope in tow right behind me. I was so sick. I was already underweight as it was and had to force myself to eat, even though I had no appetite, to avoid dropping any more weight.

I heated up some soup and attempted to eat it. I couldn't take this any longer. "Oh please, I must talk to you," I sent to Cain in a text message.

It wasn't but a minute later that Steven was calling me asking if I was texting Cain again. I hung up the phone. So, Cain was up to his old tricks yet again.

"I'm just trying to take care of you," Steven said, messaging me after I had hung up on him. He then called me up on the phone, saying, "Honey, he was even yelling at ME. He said that you were crazy and belonged in a mental institution and that he 'didn't want you around."'

Steven continued to relate to me how Cain reportedly said he'd come up there to the house and say everything to my face, yet Steven declared to him that he wouldn't allow him to. Steven then pulled up in Cain's driveway when he came home that evening. Cain was still outside working on his truck.

Steven got out of his truck, declaring to Cain that he had no right to speak to me that way. He said Cain just glared at him and walked off without saying anything.

What a wreck my life had become.

Twenty-One

I came to him just as he had
told me to, for I wished to
come in from the cold; to come
in from the hurt and pain of
all these years
I did not mean for this to
happen, but nature is as cruel
as she is relentless
The poets, scholars and
psychologists of old had all
described it as a madness, a
sickness, and a disease
I am sick with love, yes I am
high
I dream of that illogical
passion

I died inside when I heard his
words
But I said, did nothing
I gave him no response, no
retort, and no explanation
I just came home and sat
staring out the window as the
tears silently fell
Did he truly mean all those
words that he said?

$\mathcal{A}$bout a week had passed when I sat down to write

these words- on my daughter's birthday no less. Cain took hope to a birthday party they were throwing for her. I remember coming out on the porch whenever he brought her back that evening. I remember wanting to see what his mood was like.

Cain parked his truck pointing away from the house (I noticed he always did this whenever he wasn't planning on staying and was in a hurry to get away). He never came up to the house or even up onto the porch.

He got out to unload Hope's new bicycle she had gotten for her birthday and gave Steven a bag filled with the rest of her birthday gifts. He then strode purposely and confidently back around to the driver's side of his truck.

He looked in my direction as he was walking and said with that cocky tone of his, referring to the cupcakes I had baked and decorated for Hope's birthday party, "I liked your cupcakes, April." He then kept right on walking, got in his truck and drove off back home. Hope then showed me all of her birthday presents, and we went back inside.

This time period was probably one of the worst in my life. I had never experienced anything like it before. Anxiety overtook my body, and I kept feeling like I was on the edge of doing something completely irrational- crazy even. I would lay down and feel as though I literally had to grab onto something- anything- to physically keep me grounded to reality.

I was truly high from being completely infatuated with him. I could hardly function. To keep my mind off of my sorrows, I would spend all of my spare time watching television so I wouldn't ever have to think. I would drink a lot, several times a week.

A couple of days later I met Cain and Joey, who were coming home from work, at the end of the dirt road whenever I was picking up Hope from the bus stop. I was looking straight ahead so I couldn't tell for sure who was driving (Joey, I believe it was). Whoever it was nearly cut me off so I had to stop so that they wouldn't run into me.

On my way back to the house I noticed that Joey had left, but Cain was there. He was casually sitting on the front porch cleaning his gun. He was dressed real nice and looked very handsome. I remember how my heart soared at the very sight of him sitting there. He had truly stolen my heart, and I wanted more than anything to be down there with him at that very moment. I had this distinct feeling he was sitting out there on the front porch as a way to hover around to get me to come down there.

I never came, however. No matter what I might have been feeling inside or how badly I wanted him, I was not going to accept his game playing and manipulation. I was not going to let him play his games with me or run in and out of my life at his own will, leaving me to suffer in extreme pain in between. I went home and firmly closed the door behind me, never leaving the house again for the rest of the day.

All was quiet until the day right before Mother's Day. That afternoon Cain came up to the house to help Steven with a project he was building. Cain stayed around for a long time helping him. I stayed inside, doing chores and quietly reading a book, but I could see them working out the window.

When I wasn't busy doing chores, I sat on the couch. I could see Cain out the window, and I looked up at him for a minute. He was standing on a ladder, and I was sure he could see me, though he never looked at me. He seemed to be in a good mood.

A bit later he claimed he wanted to check out the trim that Steven had been working on in the hallway. He stepped in through the kitchen window from the platform that had been built directly outside it. He stepped through the window, but came no further into the house. The refrigerator blocked my view of him entirely. I had the sense he knew I was sitting there on the couch but didn't want to confront me.

He continued to stand there. A minute later he said, "April keeps everything real clean in here. It looks good."The cocky tone was there in his voice once again as he spoke. He then stepped back through the window and continued working outside with Steven.

I was in the bathroom the next day, On Mother's Day, some time around 10:30 in the morning. All of a sudden our little Chihuahua started barking up a storm. The little dog had probably the least threatening bark ever and we often loved to tease her about it.

"What are you barking at?" I said teasingly to the little dog as I left the bathroom and began to walk down the hallway.

"It's just me,"Cain said with a slight laugh to his voice. He was standing inside our home, near the front door. He spoke in a light-hearted manner. Though he said the words with a hint of laughter in his voice, he appeared to be very serious, never smiling.

"Oh," I laughed. I smiled slightly, washed my hands at the kitchen sink, then went to sit on the couch, pulling my feet up off the floor and placing them underneath me. All of a sudden Steven came and sat right in front of me, cutting off my view of Cain.

That little gesture spoke louder than words ever could. Right after the last incident, where I was down at Cain's house, love-struck and acting irrationally, I had cried my eyes out to Steven. Believing things were finally finished with Cain, that I would have no more interactions with him, I had confessed part of my feelings for Cain.

"He seduced me!" I cried as I laid there on the couch.

"Did he touch you?" Steven asked me, seriously.

"What? No. I never did anything with him," I said truthfully.

I tried to explain to Steven that day how it was that Cain could have seduced me without actually physically touching me, yet he just wasn't getting it. If Cain had tried to overtly make a move on me or place his hands on me, then he would have been considered a creep and reprimanded by everyone else around him- or worse. No, Cain's methods were psychological. No other method could have possibly been so effective at getting him what he wanted.

Bringing my mind back to the present situation, I focused on Cain's behavior that day. He was standing there right by the door, his demeanor very dominant, being both calm and serious. He had his hands right in front of him as he conversed with Steven, who was still seated right in front of me, still partially blocking my view of Cain.

"April, there's going to be barbecue," Cain said, looking at me with that still serious expression, and speaking of the gathering that would be taking place that day over at Steven's grandparent's home.

Before I could even respond, he turned his gaze back on Steven and spoke with him for a few moments. I opened my mouth as if to say something, but Cain just ignored me. He lifted his left arm high up beside him to rest his hand casually on the wall as they talked. A couple of minutes later Cain turned back to me, where I was still quietly sitting there listening to the two men talk to each other.

"Come on," he said simply to me before turning around and walking out the door.

I came down to the gathering just as Cain had told me to. I changed into a pair of jeans and a white shirt. It was a beautiful cropped shirt, one of my favorites. It had small spaghetti straps as well as pretty flowing sleeves that were designed to fall off the shoulder. It had buttons all the way down the front and parted to show off my stomach.

I learned whenever I showed up that Cain himself was going all the way into town to get the barbecue. We waited a very long time for him to show up.

Sometime after noon he finally arrived, walking through the door with grocery bags full of chips in his hands, as well as a bag full of the barbecue he had gotten. I was sitting down in a chair against a wall on the other side of the room, quietly watching the commotion happening by the front door.

Cain declined any offers for help, adamant about doing it on his own, and continued carrying the bags in by himself. He had always been that way ever since I had known him. He always insisted on making it by himself and doing things his own way. I always liked that about him.

Once the food was all laid out on the countertop, I went to the bathroom. When I came back out, I got some food and took a seat at a stool that had been placed at the table in the exact spot where I was going to sit. Everybody else was sitting around the table in regular chairs. To this day I sometimes wonder if it was actually Cain who had placed that stool there, perhaps while I was in the bathroom, as a way of breaking me down and making me feel as though I was somehow dependent on him, but since memory is a faulty thing anyway, I'll probably never know the real truth regarding that stool.

Cain came and sat down right next to me and started conversing with the others while he ate. A couple of minutes later he looked over at me. "Would you like a chair, April?"he asked. I nodded, and he continued, saying, "I was wondering what was going on. You seemed taller than everyone else."He went over to the other side of the room and grabbed a chair for me to sit on.

"Thanks,"I said, smiling shyly up at him. I accepted it from him, and dinner continued as normal as we all continued to eat.

He sat very close to me during the meal. While he talked and acted normally, he kept a more or less blank expression on his face. At one point he turned a little more towards me to speak to someone across the table. His leg was so close to mine. He rested his elbows on his legs with his hands out in front of him while he spoke. We were almost touching. It felt so intimate. He was so close to me; just relaxed and nonchalant around me.

As we sat there so close to each other, it almost felt as though we were really a couple. He was attentive to me, but not overly so. He attempted to make sure I had gotten enough to eat, and he told me there was more food if I wanted it. He almost appeared worried that I hadn't eaten enough (I was just picking at my food, it's true).

After dinner, everyone went off into the other room to talk and relax. I went into the back room to play with Hope and Steven's younger cousin. After a while, I made my way back into the main room with the others. I sat in a chair close to where Cain was. Still remaining calm and relaxed, he engaged me in some light conversation as he talked with the others.

Before everyone left, we all stood together in a circle talking- everyone except Cain. He hung back in the kitchen, never actually joining the group. I don't know what he was doing in there. He was right there facing towards me, directly in my line of vision, as I stood there conversing with the others. I had the feeling that he was quietly observing me, but I never actually looked right at him to find out for sure. I just kept talking with the others until everyone dispersed and left.

Cain stayed behind for a few minutes longer to move a lawn mower. I walked out onto the porch to watch him. As I stood there watching him start up the mower and move it, I noticed that he still appeared so serious. I walked to the other end of the porch, gazing out into the wooded area beyond.

I tried to hold back the tears in my eyes as I romantically fantasized that he would come to me, walking with me through the woods and laying down in the leaves with me. I fantasized that he would be with me; that he would spend the day with me, romancing and loving me. I continued fantasizing for a moment while I envisioned us isolated together. He would spread a blanket upon the ground, and I would curl up in his arms while I slowly drank a glass of wine. After a time he would make love to me, gently laying me down upon the ground under the open sky.

But that would never happen. Instead, I would only walk back inside, desolate. Cain came in a few minutes later, speaking to his parents and then to Hope before he left. I waited to see if he would say something- anything- to me.

Finally, he looked at me. His face was serious, blank and unreadable. "I'll see you later," was the only thing he said to me before he turned around and strode out the front door to leave, never once looking back.

I almost completely broke down right then. I was so confused. I wanted to leave; I wanted to go; to be anywhere else but there. I couldn't stand to be there another second longer once he was gone, as so deep was my hurt; so badly was my heart being torn apart on the inside.

Hope then asked for some food to eat and Betty made it for her. It was one of those kinds of things kids do to stall whenever it's time to leave yet they don't want to go. Steven's grandfather asked me more than once if I wanted something.

"No!" I exclaimed to him with tears in my eyes, hardly even able to breathe. I couldn't contain my emotions.

A short time later we left. I'm sure it was obvious I was visibly upset, but whether anyone noticed or connected it to Cain, I don't know.

Lay with me wherever we
may fall…
Roll with me in the leaves, in
the field or upon your bed…

In my sweetest imaginings I
lose myself so deeply in the
moment

To feel his strength as he lays
over me and envelops me in
the protection of his arms and
to reach for him to draw him
closer and take him in ever
deeper as agonizing waves of
pleasure wrack my body...

To ever imagine it as casual is
nothing short of horrifying...

Twenty-Two

$\mathcal{I}$ was so confused about where I stood with him. I just didn't know. Later that same day, Steven asked me to go to the store and pick up some cigarettes for him. Though Cain wasn't at home when I had come back from Steven's grandparent's earlier, he was sitting on his front porch on his iPad when I left for the store.

I looked at him as I drove by. It was as if he was looking back at me in a disappointed way, almost as if I was flaking on him or something. I drove on to the store. On the way back I noticed he had gone inside and shut the door. Was he expecting me to come down? Was he waiting on me? Confused, I continued home.

That very next evening I began drinking some muscadine wine. It was very sweet as it rolled over my lips and onto my tongue. As my mind began to blur and my body began to buzz, I thought about Cain. I got some headphones and began listening to some music. It occurred to me in that state of mind that maybe he had wanted me to come down. I had a glimmer of hope within my soul once again.

I was so confused and unsure of what to do for the next two days. On Wednesday I was wondering around outside, casually walking the dog. There was a commotion going on down the hill. Joey and a few of his friends were down there. Shortly thereafter, Joey and his friends left. I texted Cain after they had gone.

> *I'm so confused. I don't understand whether you want me to come around or not or when I am supposed to. I don't know how I'm supposed to contact you and I can't just keep wandering around outside.*

A couple of minutes later he started a small fire, even though I knew he had just burned his trash a couple of days ago. It was the smallest fire I had ever seen him build and it died out rather quickly only a short time later. Being springtime, I couldn't see much through the trees. I began to slowly and cautiously make my way down the hill. Immediately I heard Cain get into his truck and shut the door. He then started up his truck and left.

I felt so hurt and humiliated. I sent him another message telling him that I had come down:

> *I came down, but you left. I don't understand. What am I supposed to do? Please, you're going to have to tell me what to do.*

He came back home only a few short minutes after he left. I walked into the bedroom. Steven was off doing something else and had left his phone lying on the bed. Curiosity overcoming me, I took a quick look at his phone. Sure enough, he had a missed call from Cain. But

I had never even heard the phone go off. I had this sinking feeling in my gut that Cain had called Steven, only letting the phone ring once or twice before hanging up. Something inside told me that he had done it only to make me paranoid and keep me off-balance and confused. I dismissed the notification on Steven's phone. Cain never sent copies of those messages to Steven nor did he ever tell Steven about them. Once again I found myself uncertain of where I stood in Cain's life and felt very insecure and confused.

The next day I had to run some errands. It was somewhere around two in the afternoon. On my way out, I passed Cain. He was on his way home. Rarely was he ever home so early. I thought it a bit unusual. He didn't wave as he passed me and he looked very focused. He was still home, alone, when I got back.

An hour or so later I went to get Hope from the bus-stop. Afterward, we both walked down the hill to Cain's house together. Cain was by his truck doing something and paying no mind to me. I cautiously approached him, unsure of what kind of mood he was in. Over the years I had seen him in all kinds of moods and had no idea what to expect out of him this go around.

As it turned out, he wasn't mad. In fact, he just acted like his normal self with a "whatever" attitude as he continued doing what he was doing. He then said he had to take his truck for a test drive and left. Hope and I just walked around, and I let her play while he was gone.

A few minutes later Cain came back. I'm sure he knew I had come to talk to him but he made himself super-busy all of a sudden. He poured some gasoline on the gravel out in front of him. I kept my distance. He then started spraying water over it. I *really* kept my distance. He could indeed be so strange at times, but I had a feeling there was a method to his madness this go around.

Whenever he was done, I thought to go near him, yet he kept moving around constantly- both inside and outside the house. I kept trying to find him but couldn't ever catch him. I didn't even know what he was doing. It was impossible to tell.

I would go inside the house, thinking I had seen him there, but when I got there, he would be gone. I would then see him somewhere else only for him to disappear again. I then walked around to the right side of the house and saw him on the phone. He had a bag of something in his hand- concrete mix, it appeared. He dropped it on the ground then took off towards somewhere else. I had that pleading look on my face that I needed to speak to him (a look which he noticed and later commented about, putting me down for it and acting like there was something wrong with me because of it).

I finally gave up and went and sat down, leaning against a tree, while I waited. I had the Chihuahua with me on a leash. She crawled up into my lap, and I gently petted her while I sat there. I never even saw him pick up the phone. I don't know whether he called someone or if someone had called him. The truth is, I didn't even remember hearing him talk at all (at least I was never sure about it anyway).

A short time later Steven pulled up. Instantly Cain was off of the phone, sitting on his tailgate with his arms and ankles crossed looking, for all the world, like he had nothing better to do. I looked up at him from where I was sitting there on the ground. He looked satisfied. Steven then walked up and stood right over me with his legs spread apart as if he was claiming me and being territorial.

Cain looked down at me and then back up at Steven with a self-satisfied half-smile- a smirk, really. He had that squint to his eyes again. He and Steven talked together for a minute while I sat there on the ground, still petting the dog. Hope then got in the car and Steven asked me if I was ready to go. I looked up at him.

Getting up off the ground, I gently said to Steven, "I'll be up in a little bit. I've got to talk to him."

Steven just said "Ok." He then left.

After Steven and Hope had gone home, I ran over to Cain. He had already turned around to go back to whatever it was he had been doing before.

"Hey," I said as I ran up to him. He turned around, acting like he was doing me some kind of favor by talking to me. "I'll never be a part of your life, will I?" I said sadly to him.

"Oh, probably not,"he replied to me, sighing.

Even though I had already resigned myself to the fact that he would never love me a long time ago, my heart sunk in my chest. I talked to him for a while that day, and he confused me so greatly. He messed with my mind and twisted my heart. I remember asking if Steven was worth more than me. His only reply to me was to say, "Well, he's my son," and "Whatever you want to think."

"Why do you go and call him every time I text you?" I asked him.

"Father-in-law, daughter-in-law. We don't do that," he stated harshly, as if reprimanding me.

"But how am I supposed to communicate with you?"

"You're not."

"But what if I need you?"

"Then call me."

I spoke to him a lot that day and told him how I felt. He then began calling me unhealthy again for being so upset that I couldn't be a part of his life.

"I have to be here and live here, all the while being the only one that doesn't fit in. Everyone else has a place in your life except me. Why? What is wrong with me?"I asked him tearfully.

He said a few more things to me, and then told me how Joey had complimented me. He sent me on various emotional highs and lows throughout our entire conversation.

"I love you,"I told him. Of course, he already knew that. He had always known that.

"Yeah," he said, making it seem like it was a perfectly normal thing to love one's in-laws.

I then asked him if I could come in if I was upset.

"Come in how, April?" he said harshly, obviously making a reference to my last blog posting. I was upset, and he was trying to make me feel guilty. He told me I could come in every once in a while. "But I won't put up with it for long,"he said. "I'm a hard-ass," he continued, saying he couldn't deal with emotional women. He wouldn't put up with it- not from me *or* his girlfriend, he said.

Standing there, leaning up against his truck with his ankles crossed and looking quite pleased with himself, he said we'd merely say "hi" and "bye" and nothing more when we saw each other- that's all it would ever be between us.

"You don't want me?" I asked.

"Did I say that?" he questioned me back, mockingly. The fact that he never actually answered the question did not escape me. "You're imagining things," he continued.

Dear God, I thought, *he's going to deny everything*! I knew he was lying. He was so confident as he said it- *too* confident.

"It's wrong, April," he said. He was looking me boldly in the eyes, his gaze never wavering- a dead giveaway to his deceitfulness. Once again, he looked pleased with himself.

I leaned against the pole and talked to him for a while longer. We talked about how I looked up to him and how there was an undertone of romance to it.

"But how would you define 'romantic?'" I asked him as I rested my head shyly against the pole and looked up at him.

"Oh, there are so many ways," he said to me as he lowered his voice, charming me yet again, and causing me to blush and look away.

I never wanted to leave his presence. Yes, he had been awful to me, but part of me liked the way he could manipulate my mind. Part of me *liked* that feeling he induced in me; the feeling of being inferior to him yet depending on him at the same time. Part of me liked it when he would mentally beat me down as if I was worth less than he was.

I remembered talking to Steven the year before. "He manipulated me!" I exclaimed as I buried my head into the pillow, crying.

"Yeah, but you kind of wanted him to,"he said.

It was true, I had wanted him to, but it all meant nothing if he would never truly love me. I would never allow him to be authoritative over me if he could not also be real with me. There could never be any fulfillment with holding him casually for a moment, only to have him slip away from me and right back out of my life again. There could never be any lasting contentment for me if all I had from him was superficial game playing to sustain my desire for him.

Cain spoke with me for a little while longer that day, claiming that it was good that I was finally talking to him. Then he slowly began to back away, claiming he needed to pee. His feet were still pointed towards me (a good sign), and he leaned back on his heels some (a sign of someone hearing something that pleases them). I stood there for a moment longer after he had walked away. I then turned around and walked slowly back up the hill, headed for home.

He broke me; he broke me
apart
I ache in the most intimate of
places
But if my love is not returned
I will be destroyed
Either way, I live with the
pain

For what good does it all serve
if it is baseless and
meaningless?
What good is passion if it does
not exist to take away the hurt
and the pain of living?
Say you don't want me, and
I'll walk away and never look
back
Because life is pain but I can
take it
And if he says it then he'll
forever live with it

Twenty-Three

*I know that men will
play games if we allow them
to. And when we take into
account that the most heinous
of all crimes and wrongdoings
are oftentimes committed
against us by the very ones
we know and trust the most,
the portrait of humanity
becomes even more bleak…*

$\mathcal{T}$he following days were some of the worst days of

my life. My mind was wracked with cognitive
dissonance. I laid on the couch for days and found

escapism through entertainment however I could. I pushed through each day only by virtue of not thinking lest I go crazy.

My soul had sunk to the pits of despair. I was so alone and isolated. I had no one to confide in or talk to who would understand or who wouldn't put all of the blame on me. I pushed through each day by telling myself that I was strong; that life is pain and we just deal with the hurt and live day by day.

I tried to not even look out the window, so deep was my pain. I did not feel any romantic attraction or arousal. I only felt despair while I simply failed to comprehend anything. I didn't want to talk to anyone. I tried to shut my mind off completely, especially when I had to drive by Cain's house. I would have rather been physically abused, as a black eye would have been much more humane than what he had done to me. His harsh words still cut through to my very heart. I would have rather been hated.

"We've already been through this. How many times do you have to be told? You're family, come around anytime,"he said, even while he evaded me and told me he'd never contact me or tell me to come around.

He contradicted himself and spun everything around on me.

"So how did your talk go?" Steven asked me when I walked in the door that afternoon after I had talked to Cain.

I can't even remember what I said to him. I murmured something then walked off, wanting to be alone. The second I had gotten some peace from everything Cain had done to me, he had sucked me back in, yet again, for another round of mind-fuckery. The healing process would have to start all over again, and I knew it would be many weeks before I would even feel any semblance of relief.

"Yet you keep going back," Steven said.

I just looked back at him with disdain. He didn't get it. He never would- not that it mattered anymore. The passion between us had already been dead for many months now.

A wise woman must
hold back so she can see what
a man's really all about... It is
generally only when a woman
makes it clear that sex cannot
be forthcoming without a
relationship, that the gig is up
and the game is no longer
working, and seeks that
finality that the truth is
revealed and the man shows
his true colors...

The very next day I went and published a post on my blog. I titled the posting *The Game*, talking very broadly about "game" and some of the tactics men use, including the tactics of covert emotional manipulation, when attempting to seduce women. Perhaps it was just coincidence, again, or perhaps not, but Cain was then all of a sudden in a funk for weeks to come.

"I don't remember ever seeing him like that before,"Steven told me.

A couple of days later Cain came up to the house to help Steven with some construction work. He then wanted to go shoot his gun off in the back yard. It had been over a year since Cain had come up to shoot his gun off- since right after Steven had told him I wished to speak with him about the past. I often wondered if he did it just to make some kind of statement.

I heard the gun going off in the backyard. Watching depressing music videos and attempting to not even think, I had been completely unaware that Cain was out there. Hope and I got up and walked to look out the glass door, observing the men outside. Cain was in his work overalls. Again I thought that he always looked so good in them.

As he walked by, he noticed us at the door and looked up. I didn't have my contacts in so I couldn't read his expression, but I knew he didn't smile. Though I'll never completely understand it, Cain's mood just continued on like that for a long time.

A couple of weekends later I was heading out on a Saturday. Cain and Joey were outside moving some things around on the porch. Cain gave me the worst stare as I drove by. His look was unmistakable. He had glared at me, completely pissed off.

If, on occasion, Cain did come up and help Steven with something, he would hurry away soon afterward. One day when Steven was unloading some things down at Cain's house, Steven said Cain walked outside to see what was going on.

"Just curious who was out here," Cain reportedly said. "I'm about ready to just pack up and move away. I'm sick of all the bullshit."

Steven stated again that it had been a long time since he'd ever seen Cain like that. Perhaps there was something that just wasn't going well for him, Steven reasoned, or perhaps he wasn't getting something that he wanted.

"Do you think that's really what it is?" I asked him.

"I don't know," Steven said, "but it must have been something he was wanting pretty badly if that indeed is the case."

I contemplated that for a while, still not understanding. I had a feeling that I had a lot to do with Cain's moods, but I still just didn't understand the connection. Again, if he wanted me that bad, what was he waiting for? All he had to do was come for me and be real with me. I would have loved him back in return. What was his deal?

I did wonder if Cain had come out and made those statements, knowing that his words would probably get back to me, as a way of attempting to instill some sort of dread in me and getting me to come back around again.

I do admit that for a brief minute I thought about it, a dramatic fantasy coming to my mind of how I'd run and jump in his arms, clinging to him like I'd never see him again and eagerly jumping into bed with him like it was the last moment in time or something and the world was going to come crashing down all around us the very next day.

I did nothing of the sort, however. I was still way too vulnerable and instead made sure to stay out of sight anytime that Cain would be around. I would sit firmly back in the bedroom, burying my head in a book or puzzle of some sort, every time Cain would come around (which wasn't really that often).

The problem wasn't that I hated him, but rather that I still loved him. Just one interaction with him carried with it the threat of a complete collapse of my sanity. I had no choice but to stay out of sight.

About three weeks after I had written *The Game* we were coming back from the grocery store. It was raining, and Cain was outside, sitting casually on the swing on his front porch. He gave us a wave. The wave curiously resembled one that Joey might have given. It was almost sarcastic.

That very night I had a couple of drinks and went out onto the front porch. I began to pet our cat and sing into the wind. In the back of my mind, I wondered if Cain was still sitting outside. I began to sing sweet words of passion as I held my hands out into the rain, singing an invitation for him to come to me. Perhaps he had heard me?

That next morning Steven, Hope and I had a family reunion to go to. That evening Cain called Steven and asked if he wanted some materials he had run across. Steven was interested. As soon as he got off the phone, however, his grandfather was calling him, saying he hadn't seen Hope and I at Sunday dinner in a long time.

His grandfather's mind wasn't always all there anymore. Even while still on the phone with Steven, somewhere in the conversation Betty could be heard in the background asking him who he was talking to, to which Steven's grandfather only responded that he hadn't talked to Steven in a while.

I had this gut feeling about the situation and felt it was not wise to go down there the next day. The next morning we went to see the remaining members of the family off, wishing them a safe journey home.

Cain was still at home when we pulled back up into the driveway. Steven called and asked if he was going to Sunday lunch, to which Cain reportedly replied that he was.

"Why, do you want me to take Hope?" he reportedly volunteered.

"Yeah, if you will," Steven said.

"Ok, but I'm not staying very long," Cain reportedly said before hanging up the phone. Steven later reported to me that he got this vibe that Cain didn't really want to take her.

Cain showed up a short while later, parking his truck away from the house again. Looking out from the doorway, I could see that he didn't appear to be very happy. Betty then brought Hope home later that afternoon.

The next weekend Betty brought us a new swimming pool up to the house. Hope was delighted-despite the fact that she succumbed to swimmer's ear the very first week.

As it turned out, the well-house started acting up as soon as we started to fill the pool up that weekend. I was walking around outside in a white string bikini and high heels. I was out there with Steven as he tried to fix the problem himself, to no avail. He then called Cain for help.

"He's fixing to be up here," Steven said to me after he got off the phone with Cain, wishing that I would walk somewhere else out of sight or put some more clothes on.

"It's just a bikini!"I argued back at him, refusing to either leave or change. Of course, the truth of the matter is that I *wanted* Cain to see me like that. I couldn't help it. I still missed him and had feelings for him, no matter how wrong it might have been.

Steven called Cain, and in a few minutes Cain headed up the hill to help Steven fix the well. I stood there by the well, waiting for Cain to get closer. I then took off walking towards the house. I got up to the porch then took my heels off. I leaned against the railing and quietly watched as Cain pulled up, his truck pointed away from the house.

He got out of his truck and gave me a blank stare the entire time while he was walking over to the well. I observed him from afar, thinking how attractive he was as he placed both of his hands up high on the well-house as he talked to Steven and helped him. He appeared so strong and capable to my eyes.

Cain left soon after, driving back down to his house. He came back a short time later to give Steven some tools. At this point I was outside with Hope, playing with her in the little bit of water that we had already managed to fill the pool up with. Cain parked his truck facing towards the house this time- right in the direction of the swimming pool. I was still in my bikini, barefoot now.

Cain stayed there, still sitting in his truck, and talked for a very long time with Steven. I don't remember the last time when he stayed so long talking. I delighted in him being there. He must have stayed for a good twenty minutes simply talking before he finally left.

Twenty-Four

𝒯he following days and weeks were still filled with

such heart-breaking loneliness with Cain nowhere
around. He came up to the house once or twice, but he
only stopped for a moment, being on a mission of sorts,
and never got out of his truck.

That summer, on the last week of June, I
published another article on my blog, writing about
gender issues once again and about game techniques
versus love; how a man should provide for a woman out
of love, and not just because she's his newest "thing."

Though I was still hurt, I was at least more
emotionally stable at that point. The pain was still there,
however, and it was still severe. My heart was still
hurting, but there was a certain numbness and

acceptance beginning to form. Cain began to hover around a bit more, but I evaded him.

One day Cain came up to help Steven install a window-unit air conditioner. His help was needed to lift the unit up into the window. I stayed at the back of the house, simply reading a book. I never came out; I never interacted with him at all. He left as soon as they were done.

A few days later I was walking out the door when I noticed Cain driving up the driveway. I saw him and paused. I then decided to turn around and go back inside, quietly closing the door behind me. I continued watching out the window. There was just something about him. He appeared yet again to be self-satisfied. Perhaps it was only that he had gotten some response at all out of me. He stopped to converse with Steven for a minute. He then promptly left.

That following week was Vacation Bible School at the local church. In the middle of the week I noticed,

298

right before I headed out, that Cain and Joey had just dumped some leaves in a hole on the other side of our yard. They were just leaving when we headed out. The following day they were back again, pulling up just as Hope and I were walking out the door. Cain backed his truck up again in the same spot to dump some more leaves.

I walked out the door, simply keeping my expression blank. I was wearing that crop top again, the same one I had been wearing the summer before whenever Cain came barreling down the dirt road so fast. Hope paused at the door to the car like she didn't know what to do (I guess because Cain was there). I calmly and expressionlessly told her to get in.

I then got in the car, and we left. As I was driving away, I leaned up to look out the windshield to examine Cain, still keeping my face expressionless and blank. Cain was reaching into the back of his truck (facing my way). He suddenly paused what he was doing and just stood there resting his arms on the truck before him. He didn't look at me but instead looked straight forward. He had that knowing expression on his face and was making sure to repress a smile. I remember thinking how very fine looking he still was. *Yeah, he's still a good looking mother-fucker,* were the exact thoughts that went through my head.

He kept standing there while I looked at him, the sun shining all around him. Christ, couldn't he have at least gone completely bald or something? Why couldn't he have gotten fat or gray or shown some visible signs of having aged significantly? *Why?* Why did he have to still look so good? When I had gotten far enough down the road, he turned away to go back to work, an amused smile lighting up his face.

Since all the side windows of my car were tinted, I had reasoned that I was safe. It was only later that I realized the driver could clearly be seen through the windshield!

The next day I looked out the window and caught a glimpse of Cain quickly driving away down the driveway from our yard. Whenever we left the house for Vacation Bible School a few minutes later, I noticed Cain was in his driveway, getting ready to head out himself. He started coming down the dirt road behind us, yet he lagged way behind so I could never see where he went once we got past the middle of the dirt road. He wasn't home, of course, whenever we got back. He was always mysterious like that.

I still cried some, even that day as I was driving, at all of the hurt and pain I still felt inside. I stayed with the firm conviction that if he didn't want me to be a part of his life, then he would simply live without me in it. That was his choice to make, no matter how much it tore me apart inside. I knew if I came to him, or chased him in any way, that he'd keep playing games and I'd never have him. My heart had already seen enough pain and couldn't take anymore.

There is no love and there is no humanity in the eyes of the Red-Pill men. There is no higher purpose.

Women are only objects to
them and by treating women
in such a way and viewing
women in such a way they
also render themselves
irrelevant, because by treating
women as nothing but
disposable sex objects they
imply that men have no value
or worth to either society or
women beyond their ability to
impregnate females and fight
with each other over
territorial quests for
dominance. They make
themselves expendable.

The next day was a Saturday. Steven simply declared to me that he "had work to do." I went on about my morning routine, thinking nothing of it. I didn't know it, but Cain had offered him work. He hadn't offered him work for at least the last six or seven months.

I got out of the shower that morning and was surprised to see Steven's car still sitting outside. I thought it was odd. After all, my car was out there too so he couldn't have taken it. If he was home, then where was he? I called out to him, thinking maybe he was in the yard, but all was quiet.

Later I saw Cain pull up to dump more leaves in our yard. I then saw Steven get out from the passenger side. It was such an unfamiliar scene as of late, but one that I had missed so dearly.

I was looking out the screen window the entire time that they were out there. Whenever Cain got out, he walked around to the other side of his truck, giving me that blank stare of his again. He kept his focus on me as he was walking, as if he was trying to make some kind of point. What exactly *was* his point, anyway?

That next Monday was the Fourth of July. I remember feeling a bit depressed. I was sure it would be painful for me the same as it was the last Fourth of July whenever Cain had spent the entire weekend with his girlfriend. Later that afternoon, however, Steven told me to get some shoes for Hope.

I wondered what was going on. I thought perhaps his grandparents were out there or something, wanting to take her somewhere.

"So, what, are your grandparents out there or something?"I asked.

"Don't worry about it," was his only reply to me.

My natural curiosity getting the better of me, I looked out the window. Cain was outside. At this point, I began to get really pissed off at Steven for trying to hide things from me. Angry, I exclaimed to him, "Stop trying to hide things from me! It's not like I'm not going to find out anyways and then I'm just going to get even more upset."

Cain pulled up close to the house. I didn't come outside but instead observed the happenings from the window. Cain stood out there beside the porch, talking with Steven. Cain opened the door to my sports car, looking around inside and checking it out while he and Steven talked. Cain and Hope then left to get some fireworks.

I always wished that he would invite me down as if I was actually a part of things. If I had gone outside that day, would he have? It just hurt so bad to be left out like that, especially when everyone else around fit in. Again, everyone else still had a place in his life- everyone except me.

Cain brought Hope back later that evening after they had spent the afternoon shooting off fireworks in his front yard. Cain pulled up real close to the house and quickly got out of his truck, but Steven was quicker, shooting off through the front door and quickly pulling it closed behind him.

I was in the kitchen pouring myself a glass of wine. "Bastard!" I yelled at him. Cain was already on the porch. He looked up as if he had heard what I said. I was angry that Steven was attempting to keep Cain away from me. I had seen this behavior before in him and was certain that was what he was doing.

"Do you want the door open?"Steven asked me.

"I don't care. Whatever,"I said, turning back around to take a long sip of my wine. I had already had one glass that evening, nervously waiting for Cain to show back up with Hope. While I didn't really want to go out onto the porch, I did want to see Cain and see if he might speak to me.

Steven ended up leaving the main door open. I just stayed inside, still drinking my wine.

Later that night as Steven and I were sitting up in bed, watching TV, I began to cry. I told Steven that I loved him and that I also loved Cain and, apart from Hope, that the two of them were my favorite people in the world. I asked him to stop trying to keep Cain from coming around.

"If he's going to be mentally abusing me and hurting me, then I'll remove myself from his path. But stop trying to keep him from coming up here. He means the entire world to me and you can see that I've never been happy without him here in my life, and there's nothing you can ever do to change that."

"Ok," was all he said to me.

Even though Steven had said "Ok" and promised to stop trying to bar Cain from coming onto our property or from being around, I am not so sure that he actually meant it. In some ways, he seemed to be consumed with jealousy.

It wasn't but a few days later that Steven bought a brand new sports car. Hope and I went along with him to get the car. Hope and I then drove back home together, alone, while Steven drove his new car.

Hope and I got home ahead of Steven. It seemed to be taking him forever to get back. I headed into the kitchen to make myself a quick snack. I was a bit nervous, and I badly needed something to settle my stomach. I secretly hoped that Cain might come up after Steven got back in order to check out Steven's new car.

I waited for a long time. I then walked outside, sure that Steven would be coming up the driveway any minute. I finally saw him driving up, but instead of coming up the hill to our house, he pulled into Cain's driveway.

The smile I had previously been wearing evaporated instantly. I walked back inside as though I hadn't noticed a thing. Later that evening I asked Steven if he had gone down to Cain's first. He denied that he had done so.

"I was standing outside waiting for you. I saw you!"I exclaimed.

"Ok well maybe I did!"

I was pissed. I was nearly certain he had done it just to keep Cain from having a reason to come around.

Twenty-Five

What hurt the most was never Cain's rejection of me.

If he had been any other man, he would have never gotten so far in the first place and would have simply been told to go straight to Hell within a few days.

No, his treatment of me hurt so badly because of who he was to me, who he had always been. Not only was he twice my age and old enough to be my biological father, but he was also my father-in-law and the grandfather of my child. He had taken advantage of my innocence and naivety. I should have never had to worry about being seduced by him- but I was. And even if he did seduce me, I should have never had to worry about being played. Of course, I was never sure what his true intentions were, but instead of that being a comfort it was instead an even greater worry. I didn't know what it was he really wanted.

I shuddered just thinking about the events of the past year. I knew I never wanted to go back to that dark place again. I could never relive that all over again. I refused to ever return to that hurt and pain. To think that my pain had literally lasted for years, yet not once could he have ever been bothered with me.

Though I loved him and wanted to be around him, I never went back simply because he didn't care one way or another if I was around. If I was there, he didn't care. If I was gone, well, he didn't care about that either. I wanted a true place in his life, yet I knew inside that I would never be anything more than a mere afterthought to him- or at least that's how it seemed on the outside.

He said that others only see their relatives or in-laws here and there, such as on holidays. Is that what he really wanted? Did he not care that he had something rare, especially in the world we lived in, with my love for him? I wanted nothing more than to come around, but I couldn't. I would not come around if I was not important. I refused to be an afterthought in anyone's life- including his.

It almost seemed as if Cain enjoyed hurting me and playing his mind games with me. It made it all the worse to have to live right next to him. It was especially heart-wrenching for me to hear Steven talk about his childhood. One day during a conversation about his father, Steven exclaimed, "He's my father, he raised me!" He made it sound as if it was only natural that I would be considered an outsider, and never a *real* member of the family.

I left the room and broke down in tears. I certainly didn't have much of a relationship with Steven again after that. I just wanted to be alone. I still didn't want to have sex with him either. Being that he still financially supported me, I had tried a few times to offer it to him, but it was mainly only because I felt I had a duty to do so. I told him more than once that I wasn't really interested, and that I understood if he had to go out and get it elsewhere. After all, did I not fantasize about doing the exact same thing?

I had memories of Cain ever since I was a teenager. At times over the years it seemed he truly cared for me, but I just didn't know anymore. According to Steven, he was simply a "prick" to everyone. Even when I was young, he could never bother himself with me anytime I would try to reach out to him. Apparently, even after all these years, he *still* couldn't be bothered. Why had I ever thought things might be different?

Nobody could ever know how hard it had been for me to live there all those years. If only I hadn't been some stupid teenager and had a child, I could have easily walked away and never came back or had contact with any of them ever again. Not that I regretted my daughter. No, I loved her and would have given my life for her if need be. But, as many parents can relate to, if I was given the chance to do it all over again, I surely would have taken a different path in life.

If only my family had not moved away, then I could have had a place to go, but there was virtually no one left, save for Lenard and my grandparents. I had to live for all those years next to a father-in-law and brother-in-law who were not always kind to me and had many times treated me like absolute dirt. But in my heart, I knew there would never be anything better out there. All life was pain and suffering, and at least I could say that I had a home and was taken care of- which is more than what many people could say in life.

In the old days, Cain would only laugh and say "don't worry about it" when Joey would run his mouth or pull his pranks on me and be hurtful, but I just didn't believe he cared anymore.

It was only a couple months back that Steven was working on a school assignment and asked for my help. When I looked at his paper I saw how he had written about a childhood experience with his father and brothers; about how they'd all go fishing together down at the local dam. I couldn't help him with that paper. I couldn't even look at it. I just left the room, not wanting to talk. I remembered how Steven had once said that a simple "hi" and "bye" here and there was all I'd probably ever get from Cain. I died inside as I recalled how those were the very same words Cain had so harshly spoken to me that day so long ago in May.

Cain still wasn't around much after that Fourth of July weekend. He came up once or twice for some small reason, and then hurriedly sped away. It hurt so much, but I had already grown accustomed to his absence long ago.

It was approximately two weekends later, sometime around four or five on a Saturday evening, that I was feeling particularly depressed. I put on my heels, cut-off shorts and a little black crop-top and went outside. Both Hope and Steven were gone. I was alone. It was cloudy outside, and a storm was brewing. I could feel it in the air as I saw the lightning strike off in the distance and heard the accompanying thunder. But what did I care? Let the lightning go ahead and strike me!

I walked around for a few, closing my eyes to breathe in the air and just feel the peace of the outdoors. I looked towards the sky, stood up straight and let my hair flow in the wind. I had no idea if anyone watched, nor did I care. I finally went and sat on the back of the car. I remained there quietly as the tears began to fall down my face.

I sobbed loudly for a minute. If Cain was around and heard, then so be it. It wouldn't make any difference either way. It never had before. A couple of minutes later I quieted down. Cain then came driving down his driveway and left. I just quietly kept my head turned off to the side. There was no point. My heart longed to believe that he felt or cared something for me and went out to take his mind off of it, but the logical part of my mind told me he was probably just leaving as a way to throw it in my face that he didn't care; that he had a life that I was excluded from and he wanted me to know it. He stayed gone for a long time, on into the evening.

Yet another storm was upon us the next day when Betty brought Hope home. Betty commented on the storm outside, saying, "You might need to go down to Cain's house."

Giving a slight laugh, I only said, "Oh, I didn't know this storm was severe!"

She then began questioning us, referring to the last strong storm that took down both our trampoline and a large tree in our front yard, saying, "Did you go down to Cain's for that storm?"

"Oh, no, we just curled up back in Hope's room!" I said, attempting to act normal, like it was no big deal.

Betty was so very inquiring that day, not only in her words but the way she looked at me when she spoke. I never knew how Cain did it, but I had this suspicion inside that somehow he had put her up to it. I mean, it's not like Betty had ever been concerned where we were in a severe storm before- not even during a tornado.

The next evening, sometime around four or five, Hope and I went out to do some grocery shopping. Cain was home when we left but he wasn't outside. When we came back a little after six, however, he was casually sitting outside on his porch with his iPad.

He was sitting in a chair facing us. I had this feeling he was sitting outside signaling for us to come down. When we got home Hope jumped out of the car, asking, "Mommy, can I go down to Grandpa's?"

"Not today, sweetie; It's getting late," I told her. But surely God knew how I wanted to go.

The next day Steven called me up during the day telling me how Cain had gotten a bunch of furniture given to him. Cain was going to come over later that day to give us a new kitchen table and entertainment center. We were even getting a new bed!

That afternoon Cain walked through the door with Steven, carrying the entertainment center into the house. I sat there on the sofa, watching them as they came in.

After they had set it down, Cain looked over at me, gave me that same wink he had so long ago on that Easter Sunday, and said to me, "You like it?"

I smiled up admiringly at him. He had that same twinkle in his eye as he did before when he had asked me if I wanted another guitar.

It seemed as though he was finally being himself again, acting normal the way he used to. I didn't notice him going out as much anymore either, though I know he still did some. He was acting like the same Cain that I used to know; the same Cain that I had missed for so long.

He then left. I was so upset that he hadn't even said anything to me on his way out. A short time later, however, he came back. He had previously given us the wrong bed frame and was coming back to bring the right one to us.

He stayed for a while helping with the bed frame and helping Steven cut out the entertainment center so our TV would fit. Before he left, he directed to me and Hope a "see you later." I was sitting on the kitchen countertop happily swinging my legs and watching everything that was going on. It was just like old times again, whenever Cain used to come around helping and working. Once upon a time he had even spent countless hours to help us fix up our home. I missed that Cain so much.

He left and then went home to start burning a fire. At least this time it was a real fire, but Hope and I still stayed home. After all, I had heard those lines before. I had observed that scene before.

The very next day I allowed Hope to go down to Cain's to play, but I, however, stayed home. She played and watched TV with him. He kept her very late. I wondered if he was hoping that keeping her late would prompt me to have to come down and get her to bring her home.

I didn't come and get her, and he brought her home at about 8:30 that evening. He parked his truck away from the house again in the same position that he always did when he had no intention of staying. He opened the door and let her out then promptly strode back to the driver's side, got in his truck, and left.

The next day Hope came down again to play at Cain's. She came back a short time later to get her swimsuit and played with a water slide Cain had set on the hillside for her. Steven came home a little while later. Cain then walked her up the hill a little ways, but he didn't come to the house.

Afterward, I gave Hope a shower. Hope said that Cain told her she could come down again the next day, but the next day Cain wasn't there. He was gone for the weekend.

Twenty-Six

Stronger than he might have
ever imagined, I remember
that day when I turned and
fled, never to return, as my
heart and mind simply
couldn't take it anymore

I know I told him so many lies
so that he might never know
just how long I truly burned
for him

Every woman wants to
believe, as he is lying over her,
that he is real, that he is true

*It will either be real or it will
be nothing. He'll say it real
and he'll say it true or he'll
get nothing at all....*

*So kiss me so softly, so
deeply... My heart is torn and
being pulled in every
direction
Never leave my life, never let
me go
I've been dead inside so long,
I know
But after all these years I can
finally feel
I am human, yes I am real*

*So hold me in love, hold me in
truth
Love awaits, but only when
it's real, only when it's true...*

But if I run to him will he be
there?
If I call to him will he
answer?

I pulled back, I disappeared, I
was gone so long
I spent so much time in pain
I was physically sick,
mentally destroyed

But if he must wait for it,
then if that day ever arrives,
you know it will be so good...
But can one really wait
forever?

You know I'll never beg, I'll
never plead
If he doesn't want me in his
life, then he'll forever live
without me in it

But God knows I've never
been happy that way
I've never been happy
without him here in my life

It's no secret, as anyone can
see Days are devoid of
meaning when time simply
fails to heal the pain…

𝒯he very next day after I had penned these words in

yet another romantic blog posting, Cain took Hope
down to Betty's for the weekend.

It had been the habit in those times for us to let
Hope go down to Betty's and stay the night on Saturday
to then go to church on Sunday, ever since I stopped
coming to Sunday dinner. It was, however, the first time
Cain had ever volunteered to take her.

"I don't know why he's taking her," Steven said.
I had a feeling I knew why.

Steven had been down in Cain's driveway, working in the pouring rain all morning on a car that had broken down the night before.

Later as I was coming out of the bedroom and into the living room, I noticed all the lights were off in the house. I stopped and looked to my right. Steven was sitting in a chair in the corner of the living room with his legs spread out in front of him, silently observing me. I felt a chill run down my spine as the words *He knows* ran through my mind. He looked at me for a moment. Then a look of hurt came into his eyes.

"I feel like I'm losing you," he said. Then something near-diabolical flashed in his eyes as he reached into his pocket to pull out his phone.

"I'll be down there in a minute," he said quickly in a low voice. He was obviously talking to Cain. He then promptly hung up the phone.

I just continued to stand there, looking at him, without saying anything. He then took Hope down to Cain's. Afterward Steven and I headed into town. Cain was gone whenever we came back home that afternoon. He stayed gone well into the evening.

That next afternoon Steven had apparently dialed
Cain's number, by accident. He had it on speakerphone.
I heard Cain answer the phone;"Yeah," he said. He
sounded irritated.

"Oh, I'm sorry; I didn't mean to call you. Are you
over at Betty's?" Steven then turned the phone off
speakerphone, and I could no longer hear the
conversation. I never knew where Cain was and Steven
dodged the subject.

Around 6:00 that same evening we went to the
grocery store."This is a junk-food run," Steven said,
speaking of his sudden craving to go and buy an apple
pie, candy and other assorted "junk food" items.

I was saddened to see Cain wasn't at home as we
drove by. However, upon arriving at the grocery store, I
noticed a truck in the parking lot that looked curiously
like his. My heart started racing. We parked in the front,
as close as we could get to the front door.

Upon getting out of the car, before we even got through the glass doors, I could see Cain standing directly in front of me there at the check-out.

As we walked in the front door, my eyes popped open wide and I pursed my lips together. I was blushing profusely as I tried to simply focus my gaze on the wall right behind where Cain was standing.

"Oh, what do you know, it's my dad," Steven said with a smart-ass tone as we walked through the door.

Cain didn't respond, and I started smiling. Steven kept walking off in the other direction, towards the other side of the store. I followed him yet paused for a moment, picking my hair up to partially cover my face with it, and briefly looked over at Cain. It was a flirtatious action that naturally comes to all females.

Cain was giving me the stare-down again, accompanied by that smile of his- that same smile I had seen many times before. I quickly looked away and ran off in the opposite direction, placing my hands over my mouth, blushing brighter than ever. I continued smiling, completely infatuated, for the rest of the day.

That week Cain was gone all of Tuesday and Wednesday.

The next day Cain came up into the yard to help Steven load up an old plow. He didn't come near the house but instead lingered in the yard. I came out onto the porch and watched the two men for a minute. Then Steven came onto the porch and handed me the keys to his car, asking me to take them inside.

While talking to Steven, I looked in Cain's direction. He was casually resting against the back of Steven's truck, at ease. As though I had just caught his eye, he looked over towards me. He continued to casually watch and look in my direction as I stood there on the porch talking to Steven.

Steven then left to go back over by Cain. I lingered on the porch for a moment longer before walking back inside to put the keys in the house. I then came back out and stood there by the railing, casually observing the interaction between Steven and Cain, until

Cain turned around to walk back down the hill to go home.

Cain came back again that next weekend to help Steven do some various things in the yard. Again he seemed so relaxed, casual and at ease. I watched, without ever coming out into the yard, all of the happenings going on. Even after all this time, he still had the ability to make my heart soar.

That very next Saturday Cain and I came face to face for the first time in so very long.

It was a rather warm and sunny day when I decided to go to the gas station for a couple of drinks and to pick up some items for Steven. I left the house around 1:30, traveling down to the store.

I pulled in on one side of the store. I looked over and saw Cain's truck pulling into the other side of the parking lot at the exact same time. There went my heart again, taking off at a million miles per hour. I got out of the car. We were walking towards the store at the same time, meeting face to face right in front of the double-glass doors.

"What have you been up to, April?" he asked me with that same pleased glint in his eyes that he had last summer when he returned the dog to me.

"Getting something to drink," I said softly, tilting my head to the side and smiling at him.

"Steven at home?"

"Uh-huh."

He held the door open for me. I smiled and walked in, never looking back. He went up to the counter, and I went back to the coolers.

When I reached the back of the store, Steven called me on the phone. I answered, listening to his list of demands of things I needed to pick up. I turned around to see that Cain was leaving. I was still on the phone and returned to look down at the cooler, now searching for the drinks I was wanting.

I got off the phone and went to check out. I was shaking at this point and continued to do so even after I left, undoubtedly due to Cain's presence.

Though I was calm and unemotional at the moment, it would later tear right through to my heart that he never even gave me a second thought, nor even a backward glance, before walking out the store. I really was nothing more than a mere afterthought to him- worthy of nothing more than a mere "hi" and "bye"- only that day I wasn't even worth so much as a "bye."

And they look at us
traditionalists and they call us
simple-minded and weak

But childlikeness is simply a
state of femininity
It is joyful laughter,
playfulness, tender-
heartedness and vulnerability

But there is much strength in
feminine weakness

Look deep into these eyes and
see the depths of maturity and
love within them

I have never been a doormat
nor a pushover
Stronger than he might have
ever imagined, I remember
that day when I turned and
fled, never to return, as my
heart and mind simply
couldn't take it anymore

He could not protect me, nor
defend or love me
Yet untouched by him, I ran
away

"Mommy, Daddy needs your help. There's something wrong with the dog." Hope came through the door, explaining that Steven needed me outside, as our outside dog was sick.

"Ok, tell him I'll be there in a minute," I said to her. I came outside to see our dog lying on the ground, unable to walk.

"Probably going to have to put him down," Steven said to me. I just stood there, watching, not sure of what I could do to help at the moment. Steven called Cain to solicit his help to dig a hole for burying the dog, should it become necessary.

I went back inside to get something to drink for both Steven and myself. A few minutes later, Cain came walking up the hill. He was dressed in a pair of jeans and a white t-shirt, that he left un-tucked. He was wearing a hat this time. He looked so good like that. He was so incredible for his age, and still so in shape.

After I had gotten something to drink, I came outside to join the men, bringing Steven's drink with me. Cain greeted me the same way he always did. He was his normal relaxed self, with an understanding look in his eyes as he talked to me. I felt very comfortable and safe around him.

I stood there watching both him and Steven as they dug the hole in the ground. My eyes traveled down Cain's body as he worked. I thought about intimate things, of how strong Cain appeared. I began to imagine how strong he really was, and how I might be able to feel all of that strength upon being intimate with him. Was it possible that he knew what I was thinking? I blushed.

When they were done digging, they walked back towards the front yard. I followed behind the two men, treading along through the tall grass.

"Watch out for snakes, April," Cain said to me. I smiled. On my latest blog posting I had talked about how he couldn't protect me. He was obviously making a point, although it might not have been a very believable one, had he been anyone else and had I not still been so love-struck.

Cain went out into the front yard to tend to the dog while Steven went searching for some supplies. "Do you have another bottle of water in there, April?" Cain asked me.

"Yeah, do you need one?" I said, smiling sweetly up at him.

"Yeah, if you don't mind."

I ran inside, delighted at the idea of bringing a drink to him. As I was bringing the bottle of water back out to him, Cain began walking towards me. "You don't need to get all those ticks on you," he said, referring to the numerous ticks that would crawl on us every time we stepped outside in the summertime.

I gently smiled at him and looked him in the eyes as I handed him the bottle of water. He seemed so genuine and caring. He walked back to tend the dog, and Steven returned, joining him. Cain helped Steven pick up the dog, and the two men carried him to the porch where they could make the animal more comfortable and tend to him better. A bit later Cain went back home to shower.

Later that evening he came back with some soft food for the dog. I looked out the screen door for a minute. I then walked out onto the porch.

Cain was kneeling beside the dog. I calmly stood there, leaning against the porch watching him. He was dressed in normal non-work clothes now. He was relaxed and his normal self. It had been so long since I'd seen this side of him.

He didn't say anything to me now. He just stayed there, crouched down beside the dog, petting it while Steven went in and out of the house to get various items.

Before leaving, Cain even lingered by his truck for a few minutes (instead of being in a hurry to get away as he had in previous months). It seemed that he was consciously gauging my reaction to him to determine just how long he should stick around before heading back home.

Twenty-Seven

So it was that Cain was acting normally, coming around much the same as he used to. The more I wrote about loving the real him, the more real he became. He was, once again, just like I always remembered him- minus his relationship with his long-term girlfriend, of course.

But my mind was still filled with countless unanswered questions; the question of whether or not I could trust him being forefront in my mind. Everything just seemed so strange. Over the years it had always seemed like he cared more than he was willing to let on. I kept getting the feeling inside that he had done everything primarily just to get me, but I still just didn't understand it.

The happenings over the past year had simply been too big and too incidental to be simple coincidence, but what was the connection? Could he indeed have been doing it all because he wanted me that bad? But why? I just couldn't imagine why he would go through so much trouble just to screw with my head. Again I asked myself, *Why me?*

Why not just find some easy girl in a bar or some "sugar baby" he could give gifts to that would only be there when he wanted her and then leave him alone the rest of the time when he didn't? There were plenty of young college girls out there like that; girls who made extra money to pay their tuitions by being a temporary companion to some successful older man. Though I knew Cain wasn't rich, I knew he wasn't poor either.

Why did he not just give up if I wasn't "putting out" already? Why go through so much trouble to put himself in my path and organize his workday to do so? Why go through all that trouble just for me? And why did I always feel that he paid such close attention to me? I had no proof of any of these things, of course. It was just women's intuition, which would turn out to be a very powerful tool for me.

All I knew was that Steven had proven himself to me, Cain had not. Around the time I wrote of my fantasy in the garden earlier in the year, Cain had reportedly mentioned to Steven how he had "booze in the freezer." But I knew Cain rarely ever drank. Could I have driven him to it somehow? I obviously disturbed him if that was indeed the case.

I had the intuition that a lot of his going out earlier in the year had something to do with me. Perhaps it was all coincidence, just a mid-life crisis or something completely unrelated to me. Perhaps I was just crazy, but my intuitive feelings had proved to be correct countless times before.

There was also Joey, who had been doing his damndest to run me off. It's not like he had ever really been "nice" before, but his behavior over the past few months was simply unprecedented. Did he see me as some kind of threat? Why? What threat could I possibly have posed to him?

He knew about Cain wanting me, or at least about Cain seducing me. I only knew this because of what he said to me that day at the house so long ago. But why would he care? My instincts warned me to be careful around him.

The last week of September I went down to Cain's house. It had been months since I had last gone down to his house- since the last time I talked with him; when he twisted my words and screwed with my head.

Cain was working on his truck. He had been working on it late the night before as well. I had come outside to write in my journal, recording the events of the day. I sat on the back of the car writing until the sun went down.

Once it got so dark that I couldn't see to write anymore, I put my journal down. I could hear Cain down the hill, still working hard on his truck. I kept sitting there on the back of the car, and then slowly began to sing. The wind carried my softly sung words, words relevant regarding my feelings and love for him, down the hill to where he was working.

After a few minutes, someone picked up a flashlight and began shining it through the woods until the light centered on me. I looked off into the distance, away from the light, and kept singing into the wind. The light focused on me for a time. I presumed it was Cain who had shined it right there in my face. He had obviously heard me.

The very next day, sitting there at the kitchen table eating lunch, I had made up my mind. I would take Hope down to Cain's to play that day.

Hope was excited about it. After lunch, the two of us walked down the hill. It was a very bright and pretty day. I walked across the yard, heading over to where Cain was working underneath his truck.

He looked out from underneath the truck and said, "Hey, April what are you up to?"

I looked at him calmly and smiled. "Just watching Hope while she plays,"I said.I sat there watching him for a while, as was my normal way when I had come down all of the times before. I was peaceful and content- at least until Joey showed back up.

I walked inside the house with Hope to get her some tea. Cain came in and showed me where the tea was.

"You'll have to wash a cup. There aren't any clean," he said as he showed me where I could find some clean towels.

"Ok."I smiled. I then set to work washing a cup for Hope. Cain smiled back at me before walking back outside to work on his truck some more.

Hope was in the hallway when I came to find her to tell her the tea was ready."What are you doing? Come back out here. I've got some tea for you," I said to her.

I also had to pee. I wondered if Cain would mind if I went through his bedroom to use his bathroom. I wasn't sure and was a bit shy about asking. Still standing there in the hallway, I peeked inside of his room. It was so male, so masculine- so him. I stood there for a minute. Suddenly a voice from behind startled me. It was Joey.

"What are you doing?" he said to me. He had this expression on his face, looking at me like I was some kind of crazy person.

"I'm not doing anything," I replied firmly. I walked on past him to go back outside.

A few minutes later I started to wonder where Hope was. I went back into the house, then walked back outside again calling for her. It was then that I saw her walking back up the hill, towards home. I called her back down the hill.

"What's wrong? What are you doing?"I asked when she came back down to me.

She said she was going back home, that Joey had said something to her about not belonging there. I noticed Joey had shut all the doors in the house as well. I walked around to the side of the house where Cain was still working on his truck.

"You need to keep an eye on them," Joey said to Cain, right before leaving again. I was not happy.

I walked back over beside Cain."I think I've almost got it, April," he said in his normal, relaxed manner.

I then asked Hope what Joey said to her again before simply stating, "Let's go."

We went home and I did some dishes and other housework for a while. A bit later Steven came back in the house. "I don't know what's going on,"he said."Cain said he didn't know what was said so he wasn't going to get in the middle of it, but he said, 'I didn't tell her that she had to leave.'"

"Do you think that means he actually cares?"

"I guess so."

"Then why can't he just tell me his goddamned self?" Again, I was tired of it all; tired of Cain always using some kind of third-party to get at me or communicate with me, but at least the fact that he actually bothered to say something about me coming around was a start. I finished up the dishes then walked back outside.

"Is he still down there?" I asked Steven.

"I think so."

"Ok."

I slowly walked back down the hill. As I was walking across the grass, Cain was on his way back inside to get something. I just looked at him with that look of love in my eyes. He looked back. I could tell he understood that I was waiting to see if he would say something or just let me go. I stayed there with him for the rest of that afternoon, just casually hanging around or standing in the shade watching him work.

At one point Steven came to help him. I jumped in Cain's truck to turn it on for them. I then laid my head down and rested. Cain opened the door a couple of minutes later to get something out of his wallet. "Excuse me, April," he said as he reached into the middle console for his wallet. I lifted my head up and smiled at him as I moved out of the way.

He then threw his wallet down onto the seat before he left. I just went back to resting, completely at ease. He didn't seem to have any qualms about leaving his wallet lying there beside me. Of course, I would never have touched it, and I'm sure he knew that. Out of all the years I had been at his house, many times even when nobody else was at home, I had never once touched anything or taken anything. I would have never dreamed of it. Besides, I knew that if I needed something all I would have to do is ask Cain and he'd give it to me.

The worst I had ever done was to leave some crackers on the table one time a few years back. Of course, Joey bitched about it to which Cain simply laughed it off, saying not to worry about it.

Things were going well.

Later, after Cain finished with his truck, he headed up the hill to help Steven. "You can stay here if you want," he said to me. I was sitting on the swing on his front porch but decided to follow him up the hill.

He was fast. I couldn't have kept up with him even if I had wanted to. He was so attractive that day, appearing so naturally strong and confident, the same as he had that Sunday a couple of weeks prior whenever he had helped with the dog.

I followed up the hill, and a few minutes later Betty pulled up to the house to pick up Hope so Hope could stay over. She wasn't feeling particularly well, so Cain insisted on driving her home. Steven said he'd follow along behind to bring Cain back home afterward.

"I want to go! I want to go!" I exclaimed like a child about to receive a treat whenever Steven and I were alone in the house a couple of minutes later. Indeed, it was a treat to be around Cain.

"Ok!" Steven said, amused by how excited I was. I ran off to go grab my purse, and we left soon after.

We went to Betty's and hung around for a few minutes while Cain helped with a couple of things around the yard. We then said our goodbyes and headed for the car.

Cain told me to sit in the front, and then he got in the car, sitting down right behind me. I felt relaxed, silently looking out the window on the way back, catching glimpses of him in the mirror where he was sitting right behind me. We dropped him off at his house and, upon getting out of the car, he turned around to personally say bye me to me.

I responded, saying "bye" back to him as well. I so hoped that he had heard me.

That day was one of the most joyful days that I had had in a long time.

That evening I sat outside on the car again, having a drink. I wrote in my diary until the sun went down, at which point I began singing, the words sexual and relevant yet again to how I was feeling towards Cain. That night I wrote in my diary:

I loved today so much. I hope for many more days that I can spend around him. I've always been inconsolable without him here, and I would be inconsolable should he ever leave or should anything ever happen to him. He means that much to me. I didn't feel uneasy about Cain; I didn't get any "vibes" at all off of him, but there is something I do feel uneasy about though. I just don't know what it is...

Indeed, there was something that just wasn't right about the situation. I could feel it.

Twenty-Eight

$\mathcal{T}$he very next day I was searching for Steven. I saw his

truck down the hill at Cain's and began running down
towards them. I was dressed in that same white shirt I
had been wearing on Mother's Day, only this time I was
wearing a pair of shorts, and I was barefoot.

It was just a little before noon when I ran down
the hill to where Steven was. He was standing there,
leaning against a tree in the yard, talking to Cain. Cain
was sitting in a chair on his front porch, swiveling back
and forth.

"I was looking for you," I said to Steven as I ran
up to him.

Cain stopped talking. I looked over at him for a
minute to observe him. He never said hi to me nor did he

smile. Instead, he just kept swiveling back and forth in that chair, his legs spread out wide before him. He had that look in his eyes again, and his expression was smug.

The men then continued to talk about Joey's car while I leaned against the tree, just watching and listening to what was going on. Cain talked about his plans for the day and how he was going out. Shortly thereafter, I climbed into the truck with Steven and we went to the store. Cain was gone when we came back about an hour or so later.

Later that week something very interesting happened. At around 10:00 that morning I heard a noise outside. It was the mail lady.

I went outside to greet her. She asked our address, then handed me a package- but it wasn't for me.

"It's actually for Cain," she replied. "But you never know with leaving packages on the porch like that, what with people taking things and all. I always wonder if it's going to be there when he gets home."

I thought it was odd that she would feel uneasy about leaving it down there. Heck, most of the time the mail carrier would just dump *our* packages at Cain's. Nobody had ever given it that much attention before, except for Steven and I when we would bitch about it. But all I said was, "Ok, I'll give it to him."

After she had left, I went inside and set the package down by the door. In the past, I would have called Steven about it- but not this time. If I did, he would have only insisted on bringing it to Cain himself whenever he got home, and then I would've gotten pissed. No, I was going to set it down carefully by the door and wait until later to give it to Cain personally.

I spent the day being a bit nervous. Would he be there for me to give him the package? Would I have time or would Steven come home first? Did I really want to even see Cain? What did I truly feel about him?

As to the answer to the last question, I wasn't sure. I didn't know how I felt. The man didn't seem like a womanizer or anything. In fact, I had never really seen him around many women. From the way he had talked, although I never directly asked, it sounded as if he had been monogamous with his girlfriend...not that I really cared. I didn't want to know. I simply refused to be a source of sex to a man who did not truly love or cherish me for the long-term. Again, Steven had proven himself to me; Cain hadn't. I would have to know Cain could be trusted first- and I still didn't know if he could be.

At around 4:30 I decided to go down and see if Cain was home. Hope tagged along. Cain's truck was in the driveway. He was home alone. Hope continued on next door to see her friends while I walked up to the porch to Cain's house.

The door was open, and he was sitting on the couch, talking on the phone. I stood at the door patiently until he got off the phone.

"Come in," he said after he hung up.

I slowly walked into the house. "Hey, they brought this to me."

He walked over towards me to take the package out of my hand. "It's probably the parts for Joey's car," he said.

I walked over to the couch to sit down while he opened up the package. He attempted to draw me into a conversation with him, obviously signaling that he was in no hurry to see me leave. I just relaxed and talked with him for a bit.

He went on to call a couple more people for work-related purposes. Afterward, he got out some old phones. He was trying to get a picture off one of them, he said. He had three different phones and two iPads. I found it humorous to see all the technology lying about.

A few minutes later I followed him outside, climbing onto the front of his truck and sitting down, watching while he worked. He was just being his normal self, not cocky or smug or anything, and I found myself attracted to him and at ease in his presence. I then told him I had to pee.

He was very nice and said, "Yeah, go ahead."

"Which bathroom should I use?"I asked.

"Whichever's cleanest," he replied.

I went to his bathroom, but there was no toilet paper. What was it with men and toilet paper anyway? I ended up settling for the other bathroom.

He didn't work for very long outside before he came back in. I followed him back inside and sat on the couch just as before. I stayed there talking to him a long time while he randomly looked for stuff on the iPad. Unlike earlier in the year, he wasn't fake, and I got along well with him and made real conversation with him.

At some point in the conversation, he looked at me and, in a calm voice, asked "Do you need anything for the winter? Clothes? Anything?"He had set the iPad down and was looking at me, calmly listening to me.

"Well, I could use some warm clothes, it's true. And some jeans. None of mine fit anymore. I bought a pair online a couple of months ago, yet I had to send them back because they didn't fit correctly. I'm probably just going to have to go to an actual store and try some on."

"Were they too big or too small?"he asked, still focusing his attention on me.

I laughed slightly. "Too big!" I said.

"You shouldn't get too skinny, April," he said to me. He seemed a bit concerned. He was probably thinking of one of my recent blog postings where I stated that I was technically a bit underweight.

"I know. But I never regain weight." I had lost about twenty-five percent of my body weight the previous year, and he knew that.

"Why is that? Are you not eating enough?"

"Oh, I eat just fine," I told him. "I just don't ever put any weight back on."

He looked sincere as we talked. He quietly sat there, observing me, while he asked me questions and let me speak.

I looked at him then. He looked so good. I loved everything about him. I observed his arms. They were so strong-looking. But that wasn't the first time I had noticed how big they were. Even his forearms were bigger than my upper arms.

I longed to go with him into the privacy of his room and be intimate with him. But I knew I couldn't. Not then. Not at that time. It was much too soon.

I wanted to cry at the confliction and confusion in my heart. I still just wasn't sure about him. Would he return to the same game-playing that he had before? He hadn't shown he could make a relationship with me nor communicate with me. He was being nice and normal now, but would that change? Would he go back to calling Steven if I tried to communicate with him again? Would he flip on me again? And what role, if any, did Joey play in all of this? Were they in on something together? There were still more questions that I had yet to find the answers to.

I felt inside at that moment that I would eventually give myself to him, because I loved him and wished to be close to him. I wanted to be happy and didn't want to live the rest of my life having never known him intimately. I didn't want to live out my life without ever having been close to him. *Yes*, I thought. *Once the leaves fall from the trees, if he can prove himself real to me, then I shall give myself to him.*

I felt heat course through my body as I sat there with him, talking to him and observing him. I began to get flushed. It was so quiet in the house. I looked around. I looked down the hallway to where it led to his bedroom. I knew I had only to say the word and he would have taken me back there.

I didn't feel any vibes coming from him. I didn't get the feeling that he himself wanted to hurt me. I didn't really feel he wanted to play me, but it was still too early. There was still something bothering me.

I felt so much inside how I longed to take all of him in, to receive him for who he was and who he might ever be- to accept and love him. But there was also the very real fear in my mind that, especially since he was old enough to be my father, he would play me. There was a very real power imbalance between us, and despite the knowledge I had already gained, I simply didn't have the years of experience that he had. I never would.

Hope played for a long time at her friend's house that day. Finally, I saw her walking back up the hill. "Down here!" I called to her, and she came walking back down.

She wanted to go home, she said, when she got back down to Cain's house, but she wanted something to drink first. Cain gave her a pink cup (that he obviously kept there for her) and said she could bring it back when she came to visit. I knew it was his way of telling us to come back.

He smiled at me and looked at me with a genuine softness in his eyes. I smiled back at him. I got the very real feeling that he understood everything; that he understood what I was feeling and that he understood my dilemma. I truly sensed that he was genuine.

A couple of days later, on a Saturday afternoon, Hope and I took a walk down to Cain's. He was busy working around the house. He had been working outside for most of the day. He came up a couple of times that day to help Steven with some work. He seemed normal and relaxed, for the most part, but I did get this feeling that he was trying to push us away. It was like his attitude had all of a sudden changed again.

Hope was thirsty and asked him for something to drink. He went inside, and we followed him. He made her some strawberry milk but then ushered us out of the house, closing the door behind him.

"Come on," he said to her. "There are things in here you could get hurt on."

Was he kicking us out? What was going on? He had never done that before. In all the years past we had always been welcome there, even if Cain was gone. As soon as we had gotten out of the house, Joey showed back up. Could that have had something to do with it? But what was the connection?

Hope and I started walking up the hill. Hope got a sticker in her foot, and we both fell down. I ended up having to carry her.

Cain was at the bottom of the hill, in his truck, getting ready to drive up to our house. He first stopped and talked to Joey, who was just pulling in.

Cain was starting to act strangely. He was disregarding both of us and acting aloof again. When he was done helping Steven he walked off in the opposite direction to leave instead of coming over to where we were standing. It was like he was avoiding me all of a sudden. What was happening?

Hope and I came back down to Cain's a few minutes later. He was standing by his truck, and we walked up to him.

"We brought the cup back to you," we said, smiling, as we handed it up to him.

"It's Ok," he said. "You could have kept it." He wasn't mean nor was he agitated when he said it. His voice was calm, gentle even. He then handed me a power-tool and said Steven was waiting for me to bring it back up to him.

"Ok," I said softly, confused. It seemed like I was just being dismissed by him.

Hope wanted to stay behind and play. I told her to ask Cain. He told her he had to go somewhere, so she followed me back up to the house, even though Cain never, in fact, went anywhere that night.

As soon as Hope and I had walked off, Joey came out of the house. Joey started saying something, loudly. One of the two men then started laughing; I wasn't sure who.

Surely Cain would not laugh at us, would he? I thought. What kind of man would be influenced by his son, anyway?

At that moment I resigned to stay gone unless somehow fate brought me back to him. Perhaps life would go smoother anyway if I just stayed alone and to myself, I reasoned. At least that way I couldn't ever get hurt. But even while I felt that way, I did still sincerely pray that God would not take Cain away from me or take him out of my life.

Twenty-Nine

$\mathcal{T}$hat very next weekend I went shopping. Betty came

up to get Hope so she could spend the night again, as usual.

Whenever she came up to the door, Betty handed me a hundred dollars.

"Because we love you, this is so you can get you some clothes," she said. "I know what it's like to be a young woman and I know how young women are often ignored."

"Thanks," I told her. The fact that she used the pronoun "we" did not escape me. I then went out shopping the very next day.

A couple of days later Cain came up to the house to help Steven with something. He came inside this time.

I pulled on the new jeans I had bought, with the money Betty had given me, and went out to sit on the couch while Cain stood over at the table talking with Steven.

On his way out the door, Cain said "bye" to me. I waved to him slightly and smiled. Before walking out the door, however, he turned around and, looking down at the jeans I was wearing, smiled to himself. Then he left.

I could never understand how he did it, but he always seemed to have an uncanny ability to persuade others to do things for him. I had no doubt he was responsible for the new clothes I wore.

The next day was a most tiring day for me. I had just stepped out of the shower to get dressed that morning when Hope's school called me. Hope had an accident on the playground, and the nurse was calling me, telling me to come and get her.

I ended up taking her to the Emergency Room to get some stitches. It was no big deal, and after a couple of hours I was able to take her back home.

That afternoon though something weird happened. I had several missed calls from Steven, so I called him back as soon as possible.

"Hey, don't go down to Cain's today," he said.

"Ok. I wasn't planning on it. I'm exhausted," I replied.

"He texted me saying that he wasn't trying to be mean, and he didn't want to hurt your feelings or anything, but he said he had a lot of paperwork to do. So he said not to come down there."

I didn't know what to make of that. Nothing like that had ever happened before. Yeah, Cain was now communicating, but he was still doing in via a third-party. It was getting old. Again, that feeling in my gut was still there; that same feeling that told me there was just something more to it.

The next morning Cain was coming down the road, alone, at the exact time that Hope was getting on the bus. It was rare for him to be out that early in the morning. Perhaps he truly had been busy, I reasoned. He waved at me, and I waved back at him.

Before I could even say "bye" to her, Hope went tearing off across the road to run onto the bus. She had never done that before. I summarized it was simply because Cain was there. She sometimes did things like that to show off when he was around.

That evening, sometime around 8:00, Cain sent a message to Steven telling him about how he had seen Hope take off across the road. Steven then said something to me about it. We both agreed that it was probably just her being excited to see him. But what was Cain's point in telling him that?

At that point, I was just sick of all the bullshit. I knew one thing for sure; there was no room for me in Cain's life, no matter how dearly beloved he might have been to me. Not only did I not want anything more to do with Cain, but neither did I want anything more to do with Steven at that point. If it had not been for Hope, I would have packed up all of my things and left right then. I was just simply done. I was only thankful that I hadn't made the mistake of giving myself to Cain.

The next weekend Steven was driving me nuts. I guess I was already in an irritable mood anyway, and his obnoxious loud music just kept grating on my nerves.

I went outside to get some silence and fresh air. Hope followed me. We stayed outside for a while until I finally said: "Screw it!" At that point I didn't know which was worse, dealing with Steven or dealing with Cain. I decided I'd walk down the hill.

Cain was just coming home from the neighbors, having been working over there that day. I don't know if it was partly due to the outfit I was wearing or if he just didn't want us there or what, but he had an extremely serious expression on his face. Hope ran up to him and asked him to call Betty. He did.

"They're on their way," he told her.

I walked up to the porch too, but Cain acted as though he didn't want to be near me. I thought perhaps it had been a mistake to come down there.

Soon afterward, Betty showed up to get Hope. Hope became excited and ran back up the hill to get her bag full of things, Steven still being completely oblivious to the fact that we were gone.

I stood down there in Cain's driveway talking to everyone. Cain just remained serious the entire time. He talked to Betty for a moment as she was getting into the car to head out. He said he was going to take a shower. He then turned to me, before they left, saying, "Tell Steven I'll be up to help him tomorrow."

He was still so serious. He turned around and walked into his house, shutting the door behind him, before Betty had even driven away. I just walked back up the driveway thinking *what a jerk*. As soon as I had walked back up the hill, Joey came driving up. I sat on the back of the car and began to cry my eyes out.

Two days later Steven called me up right after I got out of the shower. I missed the call, so I called him back.

"Hey did you call?"

"Yeah, I was going to tell you to set the drill bits on the front porch so my dad could come up there and get them, but never mind."

"What do you mean never mind?"

"He said he'd just go buy some more."

"Oh, Ok." I hung up the phone.

Dear God, was I really so repulsive to him that he would do anything to steer clear of me? He used to come up all the time. I'd hand him tools, and he'd smile at me and be friendly.

I had once written about his soft eyes, but his eyes were no longer soft towards me. I had been holding onto the memory of who he used to be; the same man who, only a couple of years prior, would have rolled down his window when he saw me walking and talk to me; the same man who would ask me if I was Ok after clearly overhearing me having a fight with Steven- the same man who's eyes were soft and caring.

But I had to face the facts- that man no longer existed. It was time for me to accept the reality that he was no longer the same man that I so dearly missed and loved- and he probably never would be again.

Was I taking his actions personally? Yes, but not entirely without good cause. Any man who truly loved and wanted a woman would jump at the opportunity to be near her. That's why I had to face the fact, that, if at one point there was ever a chance he loved or cared for me, then he did no longer. Even though I couldn't understand how someone could change so abruptly and act so heartlessly, especially to someone who loved him so dearly, I could no longer make excuses for his behaviors towards me. The old Cain was simply gone, to be replaced by a man I no longer knew or recognized.

...You know that for
a long time I have run a very
popular blog, and I know that
you are reading- and
responding when you perceive
what I write to be about you.
But you cannot manipulate

me any longer. I waited for you. Even though you kept hurting me, I still kept giving you chances- because that's what love does.

I have loved you. I have loved you in all ways. If only once you could have shown me that I was worth walking up that hill for, then I would have given you what you wanted. I would have given both my body and heart to you. I know that day when I was alone with you I felt a flush go through me, and I wanted nothing more than to be intimate with you.

Perhaps you just didn't understand, or perhaps you did, but I wanted a relationship with you- not you and every third party in

town. You can show this
letter to Steven if you want. It
doesn't matter either way.
Though I will not volunteer
information, neither will I lie.
Though your manipulation
did hurt our relationship, it
was his own foolishness and
jealousy that killed the
passion, and if he ever said
anything now, I'd only turn
around and walk away.

I don't know what it
is, but I feel uncomfortable
coming around- threatened
even. But I know a man will
go out of his way to be with a
woman that he loves, instead
of going out of his way to
avoid her. Therefore I can only
conclude that you neither love
nor want me. If you had been
any other man then I would

have told you to go to Hell
within the first week- but you
weren't just any other man to
me. There has never been
another man like you in my
life.

   I love you, and I miss
you. I have been inconsolable
without you here. -April

Though a person can easily say "I'm through," sometimes lingering emotions and unfinished business refuse to allow a person peace of mind.

Therefore it was that two days later I sat down to pen yet another letter to Cain. It had been an entire year since my last letter to him. Even if he did want me to speak to him, I was a much better writer than I was a speaker. In either case, circumstances of late left me no other choice.

Unbeknownst to be at the time, this very day would answer for me all of the lingering questions and thoughts that had been haunting me for so long.

I had taken the time to neatly hand-write my letter, as opposed to the year before where I had typed it out. I wanted this letter to be more personal, more special. It was about 4:20 in the afternoon when Hope and I walked down to Cain's house for what would be the last time. He was there and so was Joey, although they were both inside and the door was closed.

Nobody was about when we knocked on the door, so we played around in the yard for a bit and sat together on the swing on Cain's front porch. A bit later I saw Joey's arm reach around to make sure the door was fully closed. Then he locked it. I just shook my head and ignored it. His immature pranks had already gotten old ages ago.

A bit later Cain came to the door. It looked like he tried to open it only to realize it was locked. He then unlocked it and stepped out onto the porch where we were. He talked to us for a few minutes, but it seemed like something was off about him. He was being fake again.

He said he had to go to the grocery store. It was then that Joey stepped outside. Joey stood out on the porch then stated, as Cain was walking away, "I'll stay here for a while then."

We were being treated like criminals. I was crushed. Was Cain just going to allow this to happen? Not only was I being treated like a criminal and an outcast, but Hope was being treated like one as well.

I followed Cain to his truck and Hope took off next door to go play with her friends. Cain didn't act like he wanted to speak to me, as if he wasn't going to stop and talk to me. He was fixing to get in the truck whenever I caught up to him.

"Hey," I said as I reached into my purse to pull out my letter. "Here, this is for you."

"Another letter, huh?"he said. The asshole was back.

"Yeah."I could tell things were not right and I felt threatened again somehow. I looked at him and stated, matter-of-factly, "I'm going to go."

"Ok," he replied in an asshole tone. As I turned around to leave, he said, referring to Hope, "Aren't you going to watch her?"

I thought it was odd that he would ask that, being that she was already in her friend's front yard, but I just said, "Yeah, I guess."

I watched her for a moment before turning and leaving. He was up to something it seemed like, which would become clear in only a moment.

As soon as I walked off, Joey came barreling out the door."Hey!" he yelled at me. "No more of this!"

I turned around. He had his hand up but, being that I didn't have my contacts in, I couldn't see if he had anything in his hand or not.

"Stop writing love letters to my father!" he yelled at me.

"Oh grow up you immature bastard!" I yelled back at him. "You have the emotional maturity of a fifth grader!"

I turned around to leave, yet Joey wasn't done.

"I've got your note!"he yelled."Guess who's going to get your note? I fucking hate you, you lunatic crazy bitch! He don't want you! You're my brother's fucking wife! You're lucky my brother likes you! "

He just kept on yelling, even as I was walking away. Normally I wouldn't have engaged him at all, but there was something about the pure intensity of the venom in his voice that made me pause in my tracks. I had this distinct feeling that, if I had been close enough, it was possible that he would have tried to reach out and grab me. As it was, he was firing off insults left and right so fast my brain couldn't even keep up.

I was in shock. I knew he didn't care for me, but I had never imagined that he held such hatred for me within him.

Cain stayed in the driveway before slowly backing out. He stopped at the end of his driveway and just sat there in his truck as Joey kept yelling insults at me.

"This is MY home," Joey yelled out before he started insulting me more and talking to me like I was a stray dog. "Walk a little faster!" he then screamed at me.

Once I had begun to walk up the hill, Cain finally started to head down the road, heading towards the store, never once having bothered to neither intervene nor care for me in any way.

I went home. I was simply numb. I felt nothing- not love, not hate- nothing. I knew right then that my instincts were right as the threat I had long felt inside had finally revealed itself to me. Not only was Cain trying to play me, but I finally knew that Joey played a part in it all as well. As I had said long ago; I would have rather been hated. At least I no longer had to live in uncertainty.

Thirty

$\mathcal{P}$romptly the very next day, first thing in the morning,

Cain came up to Steven's work and handed him the letter I had given to him the day before.

"You need to read this," he reportedly said to Steven. "That girl belongs in a mental institution."

Joey then came up and handed Steven some money he owed him. Cain and Joey then left.

Right as I was heading into the shower my phone started going off. It was Steven."Why did you write a long letter to my dad?" he asked me. His voice was low and irritating to my ears.

My only response was to hang up the phone. "You'll have your answer whenever you get home," I sent him in a text message.

He kept calling me, but I ignored him and headed for the shower.

While in the shower, I heard Steven come in through the front door. He then confronted me there in the shower. "What the Hell are you doing here?" I asked him. "Is there some kind of emergency or something?"

"You're not going to leave, are you?" he asked me.

"No! I'm not leaving. Why would I go and leave because of them two? I told you I would stay with you."

"I was just making sure you were Ok. He said he made a copy of your letter and that you belonged in a mental institution!"

"I'm better than Ok. Let them say what they will; they'll get no response of any kind from me," I told him. He then left and went back to work.

We talked several times over the phone that day. I told him to go ahead and read the entire letter. I had nothing to hide.

"If I had been with him I would have told you. Have I ever lied to you?" I asked him.

"No," Steven replied. He then asked, "Would you have ever left me for him?"

"No!"I stated. Somewhere in the conversation, I confessed that I had fallen in love with Cain.

"Oh my God, are you serious?" Steven asked me. "I mean, I can see you being attracted to someone like Joshua," he said, referring to one of the guys at work who was our own age, "but my FATHER?"

Was he blind? Had he never once seen it through all those long months?

"He's twenty-four years older than me. He knows how to manipulate me; he knows what he's doing. Lenard was twelve years older than my mother! The age gap between me and Cain is even more paramount. But either way it happened, so what are you going to do about it?"

"I think I'm going to go back to work."

"Fine. I'll talk to you later. Bye."

"Bye."

Later that evening we talked a bit more about it. Neither of us ever responded to Cain.

"You're a good man," I told Steven as we sat there and talked. "He's not."

"I knew he could never be real," I continued, "And if that day ever came that he ever was real, I knew I surely just wouldn't give a damn anymore."

"And if he had been real?"Steven asked me.

I looked over at him. "I don't know," I said. "But he is a lot older than me, and his age would be an issue. As I've said before, I'm sure he's still good right now, but what about a decade from now? Despite what I feel, I don't ever want to look back five, ten or even twenty years from now and miss this."

Though Steven and I never fought about it, I still felt no passion for him and I still had lingering feelings for Cain. Although I said I couldn't feel anything, there were still plenty of times when a few tears would escape whenever I thought of Cain and thought of the past and all the good and bad things he had ever done to me.

A couple of weeks later, on the day right before Halloween, Betty brought Hope home a bit early with her Halloween costume that Steven's aunt had made for her.

I was in the kitchen washing dishes. I had been thinking about Cain and was crying. I wasn't expecting Betty or Hope so early and was a bit caught off guard whenever they showed up at the door.

"Come in," I told them.

"Hi,"Betty said as she walked through the door. "Here's Hope's Halloween costume."She laid the costume on the kitchen table. I quit working on the dishes for the moment and went to grab a paper towel to wipe my eyes with.

"Are you alright?" Betty asked me.

"Oh, yeah. It's just my sinuses or something. I've been like this all day," I lied.

The issue was just kind of dropped as we looked over Hope's Halloween costume and Hope started showing me everything. She was very excited about wearing her costume.

"Grandpa will have some candy down there for you tomorrow too," Betty said to Hope. She then left soon after.

Since when did Cain care about Halloween? He never had before.

Later that evening I sat down with Steven. "Please don't bring Hope down to Cain's tomorrow. I don't want her down there. I'm just saying that for in case if he calls you," I told him. I then asked him, "He hasn't called you has he?"

"Nope. Haven't heard from him at all, and I don't want either of you two down there either, at least not until Joey learns how to act like a mature adult."

Hope and I left about 5:30 the next evening to go trick-or-treating. Joey was gone whenever we passed by

Cain's house. Cain was there, looking as though he was getting something out of his truck. We kept on driving, heading to Steven's aunt's house. There were quite a few people there- quite a few of Steven's relatives.

It was admittedly a bit early for trick-or-treating, but we were welcomed anyway by Steven's aunt who gave Hope several bags of Candy. We then sat there for a while talking.

It was so hard to sit there with Steven's relatives that day and hear Cain come up in the conversation, including talk about their interactions with him. I cannot describe the pain and the heartbreak of sitting there with his relatives and knowing that nobody knew the secret that I carried within, nor the hurt and pain. It was like everyone was just there, talking and conversing and going on about their lives and nobody could see it. What would they all think if they knew the truth?

But of course Cain wouldn't want anyone to know the truth. Of course he would never tell me to come around- at least not in a way that was obvious to anyone but me. It was obvious to me by that point that he had been very careful to ensure he left no trail of evidence to show he might have been doing something wrong. He never came to me, unless he had some excuse to be around. He never communicated with me directly. No, he would make me feel comfortable around him and make me feel like I could trust him. He would then wait for me to attempt to contact him. Then he'd ignore me and say that I was crazy, had fantasies, and should be put away in an institution.

When I thought back on it, it suddenly came to me that he had always been with Joey whenever he said I belonged in an institution. He evaded me anytime there might be someone else around. What he had done to me was called *gaslighting*- subtle and hard to prove distortions of truth and reality in order to break me down mentally so that he could say there was something wrong with me or get something he wanted from me. Of course, I never did discover what his end goal was, but in the eyes of all others, he, of course, was completely blameless. I initiated *everything* according to him. It was all my imagination, and he had done nothing wrong- nothing that could ever be proven anyway.

We stayed at Steven's aunt's for about an hour before departing. I wanted to go somewhere where I knew there was no possibility of Betty spotting us. I was going to evade Cain that night- I had to.

"Lenard will have candy over there for Hope," Steven sent to me in a text. We then headed to Lenard's.

We pulled up soon after the sun had gone down and Lenard attempted to surprise Hope by pulling a white sheet over himself and jumping out the door all of a sudden. Hope just laughed.

"I don't think it's working," I said to him jokingly.

We stayed there for a bit. I let Hope play with Lenard for a while. In the meantime, I walked out back into the woods and leaned up against a tree. Though I had hated the place, it was almost nice to be there. It was nice to know that I could get away. I needed to get away. I just stood there breathing in the fresh air. If Lenard's place wasn't so disgusting, I would have moved back in and stayed there. As it was, I could hardly bear to walk inside the place, much less eat, shower or sleep there.

I kept us there at Lenard's for a long time that evening. Hope and I went a couple more places afterward before we headed back home. I noted that Cain was home alone whenever we drove back up the driveway. Joey was gone, and Betty wasn't there either, having apparently already gone home. I continued on home, never stopping.

That very next weekend I sat there at the table across from my grandmother Loretta, who was in town staying the week at a condo she and my grandfather had rented. It was then that I began to break down in tears. I had to tell her. I had to tell somebody.

"Oh, sweetie," she said to me. She was almost in tears herself. "What is it?"

"I don't even know where to start," I said to her. "It sounds so crazy, the whole thing does, even to my own ears. Almost comical, really, like something you would read in some mystery novel or see on TV or something."

"Well if it's important to you and making you so upset there can't be anything too comical about it." she said.

I slowly began to work my way up to the subject, saying that there was a third party of sorts in our marriage.

"Is it another woman?" she asked me.

I paused for a moment then said, "No- another man!"

She looked at me in shock for a moment. "You're not telling me Steven…"

"Oh no! It's not him; it's me…"I said, still crying my eyes out.

"Is this man someone Steven knows, a friend or something?"

"Kind of…I guess… It's…He's… It's his father!" I finally confessed. We talked about it for a minute as I told her about some of the happenings of the past year. My grandfather then joined us.

"April you can't stay here," Loretta said. "If this guy is messing with your mind like that, it could be dangerous."

"I wish so badly that you guys still lived here. If it wasn't for Hope and you were still here, I would just pack up and leave right now."

"Well, what's stopping you?"

"I don't know what to do. And what about Hope's school?"

"She can go to school anywhere."

We talked for a while, and I decided that I had to do it: I had to leave, and I had to take Hope with me. We decided I would leave that following Monday- two days later. I wouldn't tell anybody. I was just going to go.

The next afternoon I stood leaning up against a tree in our back yard. I was much too scared to go near the property line by Cain's house, so I had instead walked around out back for a while.

It was a clear and sunny day, though I could feel the chill in the air that signaled the arrival of fall. I felt a bittersweet sickness in the pit of my stomach. Tomorrow my entire life was going to change. I was going to leave this place.

I looked off over my shoulder to where Hope was playing in the front yard, then to where Steven was working and talking to someone that had just pulled up. Life was just going on as usual as if everyone was clueless to my turmoil inside. Could anyone sense what I was about to do?

I stood there observing the happenings around me and looking around to get a last look at the place that had been home to me for nearly a decade. With a heavy heart, I then began to make my way back inside.

Later that evening, as I sat there in the bedroom talking to Steven, I couldn't believe the words that were coming out of his mouth.

"What do you still have some kind of infatuation or something?" he asked me with an asshole tone to his voice.

"What do you mean by 'infatuation,' exactly?" I asked him. "Do you mean to ask me if I still love him?" He was being a complete jerk, and my heart was once again beginning to harden against him. We went on to talk more about Cain.

"I don't know how I would look at you if you ever actually had sex with my FATHER. That's sick."

"And what makes it 'sick,' exactly?"

"She's sitting there in the next room," he said, referring to Hope.

"There's nothing sick about it. Perhaps it's a bit wrong on some level, but it's not like we're biologically related!" I then stormed out of the room. Steven got up and went outside for a smoke. I followed him.

"Yeah, I still have feelings for him. Does that bother you?" I asked him.

"You don't have a chance to be with someone if they're only playing mind games with you," he stated.

"Do you think I don't know that?" I was getting angry at this point. Steven then grabbed me and shoved me up against the wall. "Let go of me!" I said.

He released me, and I headed back inside, resenting him all the more. I grabbed a drink from the fridge and sat down on the couch, alone. It tore at my heart to leave Steven or ever hurt him in any way, but at that moment I knew I had no other choice.

Thirty-One

$\mathcal{T}$hat next morning I started the day off as usual. I got

up and saw Hope off to school. I then came back home and got my workout gear on in preparation for my morning workout- as I did every morning. About thirty minutes later I said bye to Steven as he was heading out the door to go to work. By all appearances, it was just another day.

Only it wasn't just any other day. I cut my workout short and then headed for the shower. Perhaps I was just being paranoid, but I thought I had heard something. Perhaps Steven had come back. Perhaps he knew somehow what I was about to do? I was beginning to get nervous.

I finished my shower then got out and got dressed the same as I did every morning. Afterward, I grabbed a bunch of trash bags and hurriedly began to shove nearly everything Hope and I owned into them. My palms were sweating, and my heart was racing. Every few minutes or so, I would peer out the window to ensure that I was indeed still alone. Though it was rare for Steven to come home during the day, on occasion he did and how on Earth would I ever explain all of mine and Hope's things being packed away? If he did come home, and if he saw the bags, that would be the end of all my plans.

I kept shoving everything in bags, placing them in the back of the house after I had filled each one. At least if he did come home for some reason, it wasn't very likely that he would go into the back room.

Finally, the bags were all packed. *Ok*, I thought to myself. *Now I just have to get everything into the car without getting caught.*

I ran back and forth, in and out of the house, carrying each bag and shoving it wherever it would fit into the car. I finally managed to get everything loaded, though the car was very crowded. I was going to have to make some room for Hope whenever I picked her up.

I knew it was possible somebody might be home next door. Perhaps Joey was home and would call Steven up reporting how I was packing countless trash bags full of stuff into the car. But I couldn't think about any of that right then. I couldn't think at all. If I was going to do this, I knew that it had to either be then or never.

I went through the house one more time. Deciding I had everything I would need, I was ready. I looked over into the corner of the bedroom. My eyes landed on the Spanish guitar that Cain had given me so long ago. *Should I take it?* I thought. No, I finally concluded, perhaps it was better that I had nothing to remind me of him. Maybe then I could forget about him and finally heal. Besides, there was no room for it in the car. As it was, I didn't know how Hope was going to fit.

Taking a deep breath, I walked out the front door, locking it behind me. I then headed to the school to get Hope.

Sitting there in the hallway at the school, my thoughts were racing. Would I get caught? Would anybody see through my ruse? I had given no warning, of course, that Hope would be leaving school early that day and it would be a few minutes' wait before they had her ready to leave.

Finally, I saw the teacher walking her down the hall. Hope was confused as to why she was leaving early. I simply told everyone it was a routine doctor's appointment.

"Can we use the back door?" I asked the teachers. "I'm parked around back and wondered if I could just go out that way instead of having to walk all the way around like I did on the way in."

"Oh, sure. Go ahead." They told me.

"Thanks."

Hope said her goodbyes to her teachers. I took her hand and began to run, urging her along behind me. There was no turning back now. We had to leave- and fast.

We had made it. Never looking back, I continued on until I hit the interstate. Not once did I stop until I hit that state line. It was then that I called my mother, just as Loretta and I had planned.

"Hello," Cynthia answered.

"Mom. Hey, it's me," I said as I began to cry. "I'm sorry I didn't call you before, but I just couldn't risk it. Without going too far into details, I'm here in the state. Hope is with me, and we need to come and stay with you for a while."

"Yes, that's fine. We'll meet you somewhere when you get closer," she said.

"Ok. Well, we're going to go in the gas station here and pee before we take off again. I better go as we still have a long drive ahead of us. I'll see you soon." I hung up, and we headed into the gas station to freshen up a bit.

Soon we were back on the road again. We drove for a couple of hours before I noticed I was running low on gas.

Oh no, I thought. I had never put gas in my car before. Steven had always done it for me. I had relied on him for everything throughout the years. Suddenly it hit me that I was really on my own. We were out here alone, and all the responsibility suddenly fell to me. But I had to be strong. I had to take care of Hope.

I pulled into the next gas station and attempted to pump the gas myself, but I couldn't get the cap off. I just wanted to cry.

"Excuse me," I said to the man inside behind the counter. "Do you have someone here who knows about these cars and could help me get the cap off so I can pump some gas? I think there might be a button somewhere or something that I have to push to release it, but I don't know. I haven't had the car long, and my husband usually deals with it, and...he's not here..."

"I'll go take a look," the guy said. He came out and attempted to help, but the cap was just stuck.

I just wanted to cry. What was I going to do? I couldn't call Steven. I had just left him. He wouldn't even discover we were gone for several hours more. I called my mother and told her what was going on.

"Just drive as far as you can," she told me. "We'll start heading your way and meet you."

"Ok," I told her and hung up the phone. I felt like a fool. I was crying at this point, and a crowd was beginning to gather.

I turned back to the gas station employee who was attempting to help me."Sir? Hey, it's Ok. Don't worry about it. I'm just going to drive on this tank for as far as I can, but thanks for your help anyway." The man went back inside.

We took off again, driving along for at least another forty-five minutes before I decided it was not safe to go any further. I stopped at the next town and pulled into a small gas station beside a crowded intersection. The sun would be setting soon.

I called my mother and gave her my location. She said they'd be there in a couple of hours. I just waited, grabbing a snack out of the bag next to me as I did so. If I was going to make it, I needed to eat something to keep my strength up.

While I was waiting a couple of local men pulled up offering assistance. Although none of them were very helpful with my fuel issues, I was offered food and a place to stay if I needed it. For all the harm it had done me, I reasoned being an attractive young female did have its perks.

After what seemed an eternity, Cynthia and Wallace finally arrived.

"He can do anything!" Cynthia exclaimed as Wallace promptly pulled the gas cap off and placed fuel into my car.

Only about thirty minutes earlier I had finally texted Steven, telling him I was gone. I simply told him Hope was with me, and we were both safe, but I couldn't stay in that place. He was worried and constantly kept asking me where we were. I told him I was almost to my mother's.

"You hurt me bad," he told me.

"I'm sorry. I never meant to, but you just wouldn't listen. I had no choice."

That night was one of the longest in my life, and I didn't sleep well. I got up early the next morning and talked with my mother about the situation. They would help me, but only if I stayed there in the state.

"If you go back across that state line, there's nothing we can do for you,"Wallace said. "We want to see that you're actually serious about leaving, but what I think is that you're still in love with your husband and that he'll persuade you to go back."

"But if I stay, what then? What will I do?" I asked them.

"You finish college, find a good paying job and just live your life," my mother responded. "Depend on nobody but yourself."

I could barely breathe. I didn't want to go back, but formally leaving him would mean being alone. It would mean doing for myself. It would mean giving up everything I'd ever known. I just couldn't do it. I wasn't ready. I was sick. At that moment I would have almost preferred death than to become the modern woman I had tried so hard all of those years to keep from being.

What was I going to do? I couldn't just hang around and leave Hope's future in limbo while my small supply of cash kept running lower by the day. I had to make a decision, and once I did, I knew there could never be any going back.

"Lenard and I will meet you at the state line," Steven was saying to me over the phone.

"Ok. Do you promise nobody else knows where we've been?" I asked him.

"Yes. Nobody knows and they're not going to know," he said.

"Ok. We'll be leaving here about 10:00, which means we should be at the state line by around 2:00 or so, assuming all goes well. I'm only coming back because I trust you and I trust that you won't hurt or betray me." I told him.

"I promise I'm not going to hurt you or do anything and I'm looking for us a new place to live right now."

"Ok. I'll see you tomorrow. I love you."

"Love you too. Bye."

I had made up my mind. I was going back. I talked with Loretta over the phone. She had been very understanding, only wanting what was best for me.

"I just don't want to see you make a decision you're going to regret. It took a lot of guts for you to leave that place, and if you go back, you may never have another chance to get away."

"I know. I'm only doing what I think is best. If I thought for one moment Steven would betray me I wouldn't ever go back. But I don't believe that he will. I trust him."

About half past three the next afternoon we arrived at the state line, parking in the same location as we had on our journey up only a few days before. I called Steven.

"Do you promise that it is only you and Lenard?"

"Oh, yeah."

"Ok, then," I said as I proceeded to give him directions to exactly where we were. About five minutes later Steven and Lenard arrived.

Steven came over to the car to meet us. He and Lenard re-arranged everything, putting some bags into Lenard's truck, while Hope and I went into the restaurant next door to use the restroom. Lenard then bought us some food and Steven filled up the car with gas before we headed out. It did feel good to be taken care of once again.

"I can't drive anymore," I said to Steven as sobs racked my body. Though Steven had been driving since we had met at the state line, we had stopped about thirty minutes back, and I had gotten into the driver's seat.

"It's Ok. I can drive the rest of the way," he said to me.

I got over into the passenger's seat and pulled my legs up towards my chest. I then laid my head on my arms and began to cry. "I feel suffocated!" I told him. "I don't want to go back there. Please promise me you won't let anyone hurt me."

"I promise. Nobody knows you were gone and if anyone tried to say or do anything, I would stop it. You're just going to stay in the house and rest and recover for a while, and I'll take care of getting Hope to school."

"Ok," I said. "I'm ready."

I tried to just breathe and remain calm as we headed back towards the house. I noticed Cain's truck parked in his driveway as we were coming back home. Joey wasn't there. For a moment all the same feelings and emotions came rushing back to me. I had the brief thought of ...*if only*...race through my head.

We continued on home, and Steven and Lenard unloaded the things. Everything was such a wreck. I just piled everything on the couch, organizing it as best as possible for the time being.

Lenard stayed around for a few minutes to talk before heading back home. Steven and I then went to settle down for the evening.

Coming out of the bathroom later that evening, my heart began to soften. It's like Steven had been my protector and I was relying on him to take care of me once again. I felt my body relax down below as desire began to fill me.

Hope had already been put to bed. The lights were all off, save for a couple of scented candles burning. I walked over to Steven, gently touching him. I was signaling my desire with my eyes as I slowly took my top off and led him towards the bed. For the first time in what seemed like forever, I allowed Steven to make love to me that night. As I continued to run my fingers through his hair, I leaned up and whispered the words "I trust you" into his ear.